# MARRIAGE
# GOD'S
# WAY

*Empowerment for a Fulfilling Love Relationship!*

I0026976

## MILDRED SENQUIZ-FIGUEROA, Ph.D.

SHATARU PRESS
*Guidance for Living*
Lorain, Ohio

# MARRIAGE GOD'S WAY

This book and others by Shataru Press may be ordered through booksellers or by contacting: www.shatarupress.com

Published by Shataru Press
Printed in the United States of America

First Edition: July, 2014

ISBN: 978-0-692-24589-7


Cataloging Information:
Senquiz-Figueroa, Mildred, 1953
1.Marriage-Religious Aspects-Christianity
2.Relationships

# DEDICATION

*To David, my beloved and best friend*
*My children, Tabitha and Reuben, my miracles,*
*precious gifts from God;*
*My children-in-love, Samuel and Amarily,*
*blessings beyond words.*

# ACKNOWLEDGEMENTS

I wish to express praise and thanksgiving to God for placing this project in my heart and for giving me the strength, wisdom and guidance to carry it out; for placing people in my path to help me and make it possible; and for lovingly walking this journey with me. My deep and loving gratitude to my husband David for his assistance, support and encouragement in this endeavor and for being the man I needed by my side. His love and patience are endless and he is a constant source of strength and inspiration.

I am thankful for my family, friends and spiritual associates who have helped me in this undertaking. I salute my parents who instilled in me the importance of pursuing an education and achieving my dreams. I also salute my children, my daughter, Vanessa for the lessons she gave me on patience and perseverance. She persevered until God called her home. The time she was here was an inspiration. My daughter Tabitha for her kindness, her tenacity and hard work helping me with this project, and my courageous, unselfish, and enchanting son Reuben; all three gifts from God who have inspired me to be the best that I can be.

I express my gratitude to Brother James Perales for his work on the cover and Pastor Norva Ross for her friendship and support during the process of this project. Also, thank you to Dr. Curtis Brown for his guidance and encouragement.

# CONTENTS

# INTRODUCTION

This book is intended to be a manual or guide for couples planning their lives together, for couples working on improving their marriage and for Pastors and counselors who counsel on marriage. It presents tips and pointers from extensive research and forty years of experience in marriage. It is a practical guide to help you realize the full potential for happiness that can be found in marriage. A wedding is not a marriage. It's the beginning of a relationship that may or may not develop into a marriage. Your marriage is important because so much depends on it.

Happy family life is the backbone of a healthy neighborhood, government and church life. As the family is so are all other communities. Your own happiness is closely connected with what you give and find in marriage. The marriage promises you the greatest measure of earthly happiness but this happiness is realized only if true love and the unselfish spirit of perfect sacrifice and service guide your every action. True love makes you want to bring happiness to your partner in marriage. Happiness is a by-product of duty and love. When you try to make the other happy you suddenly realize that you are happy yourself. Christ taught this lesson long ago: "Whoever finds their life will lose it, and whoever loses their life for my sake will find it." (Mathew 10:39)

Love intensifies joys and lessens sorrows. Loneliness is the great anguish of man and you are not alone in marriage. You cannot be unhappy in the midst of those who love and care for you. In the security of love you can grow as a person. The purpose of this book is to help you know and love; to know yourself and each other as well as the privileges and responsibilities of marriage.

These times present many challenges for marriages, ministries and marriages in ministry. God created marriage for the human race. Marriage was designed to provide love, intimacy, recreation, fellowship, and procreation, in other words companionship. The only true marriage expert is God and He has shared His knowledge with us in the Bible. "Before cities and governments, business and industry, society and culture, marriage was the primary activity of mankind."

God provided marriage in His grace to bless us with an intimate and fulfilling love relationship. It is an unconditional commitment into which a man and a woman enter for life. Marriage is the union of two people who promise to stay together, create a family together and be together; who promise to listen to each other, speak to each other, keep calm, change what needs to be changed, build each other up and strengthen the love for each other.

Couples can learn to communicate, to resolve conflicts creatively, to affair proof their marriage and to protect themselves and their marriage from the influence of technology. How to deal with stress and avoid stressors, how to manage money and plan their future, but what couples really need in order to achieve these things is "a commitment to growth, and the will to make their marriage work."

Commitment requires you to give up the childish dream of being unconditionally accepted by your partner and to stop expecting that partner to fulfill all your needs and make up for all your childhood disappointments. It means that you expect to be disappointed by your partner at times and that you learn to accept this and not use it as a reason to pull the plug. Commitment is more than maintaining; it is more than continuing to stick it out and suffer with a poor choice of a spouse. Commitment is investing—working to make the relationship grow; it means working toward change. This resource is designed to help couples achieve their goals and work out a good, fulfilling and satisfying marital relationship and to maintain it.

Very few of the materials and concepts used in this manual are completely original with the author. They are a compilation, a distillation, a revision, and an adaptation of materials and ideas from innumerable sources.

My husband David and I have spent the last 22 years of our 38 years of ministry working with Christian leaders and with couples to guide them in God's purpose of marriage. We have been married for over 40 years and have learned from trial and error. We have read and studied excellent articles and books on marriage and have searched the Scriptures for guidance. Our mission has been to build strong families by strengthening their marriage relationship.

All Christian couples have a number of things in common. They love God, they want to serve Him and they long to minister to each other. My husband and I can identify with Jake and Melissa Kircher's comment "We have all learned some valuable lessons about building a healthy marriage. "We aren't perfect, but we've matured individually and as a couple because of each mess, problem, heartache, and obstacle we've encountered."

We understand struggles and frustrations, because we also have struggles and frustrations. Everyone needs to understand that marriage takes time and effort. We have dedicated years of study on marriage; what makes it work and what things can cause its demise. Marriage should be viewed as a ministry in which the spouse is lovingly served and the other reciprocates. They should both regard marriage as an arena in which ministry takes place. Being married means ministering to each other. There is no room in marriage for selfishness and un-forgiveness. Marriage and ministry both operate on the same principle of loving service. This service should not conflict, compete, or counteract. Adam and Eve had a sole focus-each other. In Galatians 5:13, Paul admonishes:

> "You, my brothers and sisters, were called to be free.
> But do not use your freedom to indulge the flesh,
> rather, serve one another humbly in love."

His admonition is applicable to both marriage and ministry because it speaks to all dimensions of the life to which we have been called. A study by D. L. Fennell reveals that happy couples who have been married for a significant period of time state that faith in God and spiritual commitment has been the most important quality of their marriage success.

Maranatha Life's Lifeline for Pastors listed statistics gleaned from various sources such as Pastor-to-Pastor; Focus on the Family, Ministries Today, Charisma Magazine, Campus Crusade for Christ and the Global Pastors Network. They reflect the danger that ministries and marriages are in. "How can we handle the ups and downs of marriage without becoming a discouraging statistic?" I will attempt to answer these questions with suggestions and advice collected through my research. I will begin by defining God's purpose for marriage. We need to understand this in order to make our marriage the best it can be. Marriage is a gift; a call to servant hood, a call to friendship, a call to suffering; it is a refining process to be refined by God, it involves intimacy in all areas; Intimacy in spiritual, intellectual, social, emotional and in the physical.

# CHAPTER I

## GOD'S PURPOSE FOR MARRIAGE

Two lives must blend in in the deepest possible way into a new unit in order for a marriage to be successful. God's idea is that they will blend and both will satisfy each other and serve the purpose of God in the highest possible manner." God has a purpose, and we should align ourselves with His design and His will as it is revealed in His Word.

Loneliness and isolation are contradictions to the purpose in God's creative act. We must first form a foundation that is the divine purpose for marriage in order for us to then process and understand the roles, reasons, and successful growth of marriage. God also created marriage for completeness. The woman was to be a helper fit for him. J. Lee Jaegers, PhD. quotes Thomas R. Condron from the thesis The Biblical Meaning and Purpose of Marriage.

> ". . . three of the leading proposals for God's intention for marriage, are: God's purpose is a functional purpose; God's purpose is a sacramental purpose; and God's purpose for marriage is a transformational or sanctifying purpose. First there is the purpose of companionship, second, that of procreation, and thirdly, that of sexual fulfillment."

God also created marriage for completeness; the woman was to be a helper fit for him. Marriage involves man and woman being fitted together for the function of mutual fellowship, encouragement, understanding, the reproduction of children, and the physical and spiritual aspects of sexual satisfaction. During the creation in the Bible, the only thing that the LORD God said was not good: "The LORD

God said, "It is not good for the man to be alone. I will make a helper suitable for him." (Genesis 2:18)

## Completeness—Children

He then created woman to complete him and meet his needs of community. Man needed someone to fill the loneliness, to communicate with, to fellowship with and to share his thoughts, hopes and dreams with; someone who would procreate. The woman assists man in making his life (and hers) complete. She fills up the empty places. She shares his life with him and draws him out of himself into a wider area of contact through the involvement they have with one another.

The partners in a marriage relationship are actually fulfilling God's purpose of completeness, or wholeness in life. God put Adam to sleep and created a woman from one of Adam's ribs; "Then Adam said "this is now bone of my bones and flesh of my flesh; she shall be called 'woman,' for she was taken out of man." (Genesis 2:23).

The second part is found in Genesis 1:28, where Condron claims that from the beginning it was in the purpose of marriage that the man and wife should have children. God blessed them and said to them, "Be fruitful and multiply!" And lastly, for the final part of this three-fold purpose of marriage Paul states in 1 Corinthians 7:2, that to prevent man (male and female) from being tempted by sin, "But since sexual immorality is occurring, each man should have sexual relations with his own wife, and each woman with her own husband."

God knows what is best for us and for every area of our lives, including our marriage. He created male and female. He created our bodies and minds designing differences as to the way we think and act. The Holy Bible tells us, ". . . Then the LORD God formed a man from the dust of the ground and breathed into his nostrils the breath of life, and the man became a living being." (Genesis 2:7)

1 Corinthians 7:5 states that the lack of normal marital relations is an avenue of attack by Satan resulting in lack of self-control. So sex, which God created solely for marriage, is not only for the purpose

of procreation, but for satisfying natural sexual desire. Therefore, for mankind to have their natural desire for companionship met, marriage had to be created. For the reproduction of the human race to occur, marriage had to be contrived; and for mankind's God-given sexual drives to be met, marriage had to be designed. God's purpose for marriage is one of function: providing companionship (Genesis 2:18-25), children (Genesis 1:28), and the fulfillment of sexual needs to prevent sin (1 Corinthians 7:2).

### Sacrament—Covenant

Covenant is relationship! It requires both parties to uphold moral and legal faithfulness to the covenant for a lifetime, thereby uniting the individuals as one. "Relationship" in its very definition carries the fact that there is mutual caring and moral obligations between each party, and the fulfilling of needs within each other. Simply because there is a relationship, they are in covenant. Biblical marriage is a sacred covenant between three people: a man, a woman, and God.

Put God First: Don't leave God out. When we put God first in our marriages, we take out the guess work of trying to figure out alternatives when things fall short of our expectations. The closer husbands and wives get to God, the closer they get to each other. Strong marriages and families are built when both spouses are directed by the Holy Spirit and work in understanding and cooperation with one another. Pray together and enjoy your marriage more. Worship together, stay together. Serve together. God is committed to help. He promises that, if we will come to Him, He will give us the grace we need.

According to Dr. David Foster in the article Covenant: The heart of the Marriage Mystery; Covenant is the fundamental tool that God has designed to construct and order His relationship with man. Covenants are established by making an oath that creates kinship between the two persons who are making the covenant. The second possibility for God's purpose for marriage is one of sacrament. The covenant made between a husband and a wife points to, or reflects, a much grander covenant between Christ and the church, according to Ephesians 5:22-33. In verse 31, Paul quotes Genesis 2:24,

> "That is why a man leaves his father and mother and is united to his wife, and they become one flesh."

We can interpret Paul's words as saying that marriage (the covenant involved in leaving father and mother and being united to a spouse) is patterned after Christ's covenant commitment to his church. Paul recognized his ministry as gathering the bride as he indicates in 2 Corinthians 11:2:

> "I am jealous for you with a godly jealousy. I promised you to one husband, to Christ, so that I might present you as a pure virgin to him."

Marriage was designed by God most importantly, to be a parable of the way Christ loves his church and the way the church loves and follows Christ. Marriage exists for God's glory. It exists to display God. Looking at the passage in Ephesians we can see how: Marriage is patterned after Christ's covenant relationship to the church. And therefore the highest meaning and most ultimate purpose of marriage is to put the covenant relationship of Christ and his church on display. That is why marriage exists.

The love that binds husband and wife portrays something magnificent—Christ's love for His people. Dwight Small supports this purpose and describes it as such:

> "To the Christian, marriage is the means to the fulfillment of divine ends. The marriage union, like man himself, is designed for the glory of God, and for the exhibition of His purposes of love on earth . . . marriage was instituted as an earthly symbol of the spiritual relation between God and man."

### Sanctification

Gary Thomas explains the third possible divine purpose for marriage as one of sanctification. He explains it this way: "What if God had an end in mind that went beyond our happiness, our comfort, and our desire to be infatuated and happy in our marriage as if the world were a perfect place? What if God designed marriage to make us holy more than to make us happy? God designed marriage to provide: partnership, spiritual intimacy and the ability to pursue God—together" Philippians chapter 2 is also used as scriptural support for this divine purpose for marriage, which recognizes God's intentions to shape and mold His people into becoming the servant-rulers that He created us initially to be in Genesis 1:26-30, denying ourselves and our selfish ambitions for the sake of considering others more important.

"Marriage calls us to an entirely new and selfless life." Entering into the covenant of marriage with another sinful, desperately depraved human being forces one to face character issues that they could possibly never run into elsewhere. This lifetime commitment of providing emotional, physical, and spiritual intimacy and care for another uncovers who you are as your true self. As Rabbi Aryeh Pamensky says, "ultimately revealing your unique purpose for being created." Thomas summarizes the foundation of his book before moving into the implications that are the result of looking at marriage through the lens of holiness as follows: "I guess what I'm after is a quieter fulfillment, a deeper sense of meaning, a fuller understanding of the purpose behind this intense, one-on-one, lifelong relationship. As a person who believes primary meaning comes from a relationship with God, I want to explore how marriage can draw me closer to God . . . ."

"Just as celibates use abstinence and religious hermits use isolation, so we can use marriage for the same purpose—to grow in our service, obedience, character, pursuit, and love of God."

God's purpose for marriage was entirely about reflecting something much greater, Christlikeness. So the third proposal for the divine purpose for marriage is one of sanctification purposes in that it was instituted by God to make His people more like Himself.

Reb Bradley argues that: "God's primary purpose for marriage is to use it to help shape us into the image of His Son." Marriage was patterned after Christ's relationship to the church. God has created marriage with an even more fantastic purpose—to direct us towards Himself and to shape us into the image of His Son. As Bradley alludes to below, a major theme of Scripture is the sanctification of God's people which meets our greatest need of becoming like Christ, drawing us into Himself:

> "The challenges offered in marriage are capitalized on by God to help shape and mold us into the image of Jesus . . . . God knows that as we grow into the image of Jesus our greatest needs are met." We endure trials, we enjoy blessings, and we are given experiences as challenges offered through marriage for the intimate purpose of leading us to God and the grace and mercy that He bestows upon His people."

Marriage is a God-ordained institution that was created with the purpose of conforming us into the image of Christ. The joys, difficulties, and challenges of marriage refine our character and strengthen our faith in God. God's primary purpose of marriage is to transform His people into the likeness of His Son. "So when the bills pile up, communication breaks down and you're just plain irritated with your husband or wife, Thomas offers these reminders to help ease the tension:

> God created marriage as a loyal partnership between one man and one woman.
>
> - Marriage is the firmest foundation for building a family.
> - God designed sexual expression to help married couples build intimacy.
> - Marriage mirrors God's relationship with His people.

This is seen throughout the Bible. Jesus refers to Himself as the "bridegroom" and to the kingdom of heaven as a "wedding banquet." God's purposes for marriage extend far beyond personal happiness.

Gary Thomas states in his book Sacred Marriage that "God did not create marriage just to give us a pleasant means of repopulating the world and providing a steady societal institution to raise children, He planted marriage among humans as yet another signpost pointing to His own eternal, spiritual existence."

# CHAPTER II

## FOUNDATION BUILDERS IN MARRIAGE

Every couple wants to have the type of marriage that God will bless. To achieve this it is important to work on marriage God's way. "On top of the foundation of love and commitment, there needs to be trust, conscious attention to your partner, and mutual respect. With these building blocks placed upon a solid foundation, your relationship will always be strong."

Paul Chappel shared a message from Dr. Paul Kingsbury. The message dealt with the three kinds of biblical love needed in a marriage. "We were challenged to have a God love, a friendship love and a romantic love." Christian couples who diligently work to strengthen their homes and commitments to one another should be respected and emulated. We must emphasize having God's love in our marriages. With all of the hustle and bustle of everyday life, every married couple must set time aside to develop the three kinds of biblical love. "Our marriages and our families are our first ministry and they should be the most important ministry in our lives.

Stress fractures can occur when we do not take time to cultivate godly love in our marriages. Sometimes these stress fractures lead to complete brokenness." Today's lifestyle leads to the neglect of the family for the sake of self; family and the relationship with God has moved to last place.

There really are "keys" and time-tested principles which can help produce truly JOYOUS marriages! Our success in marriage depends upon our willingness to USE these keys in our own lives. History shows us that any nation whose society allows or causes its families to come apart soon begins to disintegrate. Most historians note that "the breakdown of the family" was one of the symptoms, if not causes, of the fall of the Roman Empire.

Here we have some words of wisdom on marriage. The first one is the Holy Bible's words of wisdom inspired by God and written by Solomon. Solomon was said to be a great man of wisdom:

> "Unless the LORD builds the house, the builders labor in vain" (Psalm 127:1)

The following quotes are by two of our country's former presidents:

> "Strong families are the foundation of society. Through them we pass on our traditions, rituals and values. From them we receive the love, encouragement, and education needed to meet human challenges. Family life provides opportunities and time for the spiritual growth that fosters generosity of spirit and responsible citizenship." Ronald Reagan

> ". . . unless we work to strengthen the family . . . to create conditions under which most parents will stay together—all the rest: schools, and playgrounds, and public assistance, and private concern, will never be enough to cut completely the circle of despair and deprivation." Lyndon B. Johnson

A marriage can last a lifetime. Most of the lessons our kindergarten teachers drilled into us as children are also useful in our adult relationships. Treating others the way we'd like to be treated with kindness, fairness and respect seems simple enough. Be kind, not nice. But niceness is one rule that can actually backfire in a romantic relationship. Some partners can (however wrongly) interpret niceness as weakness. Moreover, niceness is often insincere—it is a coping mechanism taught to us as children to help us deal with people we don't really like. True kindness, by contrast, doesn't pretend. Kindness looks to the core worth of another person and responds accordingly. Kindness doesn't mean avoiding conflict or even always "playing nice"—it just means processing through issues with a sincere respect for your spouse's feelings and humanity.

## Build on a Solid Foundation

Marriage cannot withstand the storms of life without a solid foundation. Recognize God as the expert. Focus on companionship. Complement each other. Prioritize the relationship. Husbands need to step up and lead. Form an independent union and bond to each other. Develop deep intimacy and be vulnerable and accepting. God established that marriage as a covenantal work, whereby He Himself enters into the union and pledges His help and support.

Prioritize the relationship. Determine to make it permanent.

## Love and Respect

We believe love best motivates a woman and respect most powerfully motivates a man. Research reveals that during marital conflict a husband most often reacts when feeling disrespected and a wife reacts when feeling unloved. If you want your mate to feel loved, learn to speak his or her love language. Say it with words and with touch. Say it with time together, with helping out, with material things and with loyalty. Say it with meeting emotional needs and say it with bringing out the best. Remember, it was your differences that first attracted you to your mate. Wise marriage partners understand and appreciate their differences.

Always show as much courtesy to your partner as you would a stranger. Show respect and affection for each other. When a couple fails to respect each other, they often slip into negative habits. Research shows that nothing can damage a relationship quicker than criticisms and put-downs. Treating your partner as you would like to be treated will do a lot to strengthen the bond between you. Paying your partner a compliment is a quick and easy way to show him or her respect. When you are tempted to complain to someone about one of your partner's flaws, ask yourself how you would feel if he or she did that to you.

True love certainly involves deep and abiding respect. A man ought to be grateful and thankful that the woman who is his wife has decided to cleave to him above all others unto death. He ought to appreciate that fact—and the many, many good qualities of help, patience and service, which practically every wife possesses. He ought to encourage and bring out the best in her—not constantly harp away at her in belittling criticism.

## Meet Your Mate's Need

God created marriage and he also created men and women. Men and women have different emotional priorities, and trying to understand is crucial to a happy union. God knows that men need unconditional respect and women have a primary need for unconditional love. Man needs admiration, woman needs attention. He needs approval, she needs affection. As you invest in your mate by making efforts to meet his or her relationship needs, your feelings of compassion (good will) for your mate naturally increase, and your mate naturally feels more attraction for you.

This increased desire helps motivate your mate to meet your relationship needs, and the feelings of compassion and attraction become mutual. This is how romantic love grows in a marriage. Wives, if you want more love, show more respect. Husbands, if you want more respect, show more love. Love is expressed by seeing a need and extending yourself to meet it.

## Be understanding

By understanding your spouse's feelings, you will ease frustration, strengthen your marriage and increase your happiness.

## Ignite the Romance

Marriage is intended to be a passionate, vibrant, intimate adventure. Express love fully and frequently. Enjoy intimacy thoroughly. Husbands, your wives need romance. Wives, your husband needs responsiveness . . . spontaneity, creativity, unpredictability are the fuels to spark the romantic fires! When husbands focus on being more romantic, and wives focus on being more responsive, romance is ignited, passion is renewed and love is deepened. Your goal is to innovate in your relationship! Be spontaneous, creative and unpredictable!

## Be attractive

Improving your marriage by being someone who your partner feels enticed to be around is one of the most important things you can do for your relationship. You need to appear more attractive physically and spiritually. Be compassionate. Compassion stretches you emotionally and says to someone you are capable of connecting deeply. And be steadfast to your core principles. People admire integrity and courage. Be consistent in your principles and actions.

## Fill Your Mate's Love Tank

After the first or second year of marriage, when the initial "tingle" is starting to fade, many couples find that their "love tanks" are empty. They may have been expressing love for their spouse, but in reality they may have been speaking a different love language. The best way to fill your spouse's love tank is to express love in their love language. Each of us has a primary love language.

Usually, couples do not have the same love language. Dr. Gary Chapman recommends that you have a "Tank Check" 3 nights a week for 3 weeks. Ask one another "How is your love tank tonight?" If, on a scale from zero to ten, it is less than 10, then ask "What can I do to help fill it?" Then do it to the best of your ability. Encourage and build up your mate. Sincere, positive, and encouraging comments will add to your mate's love tank.

Negative, insincere, or discouraging comments, or not saying anything at all, will draw your mate's love tank. Make a list of your mate's positive qualities, things you especially appreciate. Honor your mate by showing respect, admiration, esteem, reverence, consideration, recognition and appreciation. Honoring your mate is a matter of making him or her feel important.

The deepest urge in human nature is the desire to feel important. Help carry your mate's burden. Listen to him or her. Pray for and with him or her. Serve your mate. Serving is doing those little things that make the other person's life easier. Be sensitive to your mate, humble, kindhearted and compassionate to one another. Hurt people hurt people. Go to God to get your tank filled so that you can fill the tanks of those you love.

## Connect with your Spouse's Heart

Care for your spouse's heart: Connect by understanding. Talk less, listen more. Give your mate your full attention. Fight for your spouse's heart. Ask God to open the eyes of your heart toward your spouse and give you compassion for him or her. Look for unspoken fears, concerns, moods and aspirations. Respect how valuable and vulnerable your spouse's heart is by treating it gently. Connect by understanding and giving your full attention. Listen without thinking about how you are going to respond. Make your mate feel important and express gratitude.

Connect by building togetherness sexually, intellectually, sharing in creative arts, sharing fun and play. Connect in crisis intimacy by going through hard issues together (real problems and pain together). Even conflict unity is possible by facing and struggling through differences effectively together and spiritual intimacy is gained by growing closer to God in an ongoing partnership. Connect by continuing to date. Some ideas are to go on a walk in a park, browse in a bookstore, go to a play or a musical, go out for ice cream, watch a movie, attend a sports event together, double date with some friends or make it a special night at home and cuddle together.

Marriage needs to be built on a solid foundation; God needs to be first. Couples need to fulfill their vows, understand their mate and celebrate their differences. V.L. Hamlin a writer in Yahoo! Contributor Network, shares four marriage tips which have helped her grandparents marriage last for over 50 years.

**Marriage Tip # 1**

"Don't forget who you married and don't forget why you married! What was he/she like when you married, what are the reasons that you married him/her? Really think about these two questions! What was it about your spouse that made you fall in love with him/her? Were they funny, caring, loving, romantic . . . what were the reasons? Thinking about this will help you remember the person you fell in love with.

**Marriage Tip # 2**

ARGUE! It is okay to disagree. Now, I'll bet you are surprised to see that one here! It is human nature to have feelings of anger or resentment. You need to share your feelings with your spouse even if you feel anger, especially if it is directed at him/her. Do not forget to let him know why it bothers you that he did not do what he should have done! If you don't share your feelings and the reasons for your feelings, you are not communicating and without communication a marriage is bound to fail.

**Marriage Tip # 3**

Acknowledge and accept each other's faults. We all have them, so why hide them? Everyone has their own pet peeves about annoying things, but the trick is to acknowledge the things that aggravate you and accept them as what they are . . . pet peeves. They aren't really harming anything and if you think back, it's probably something you thought was cute or funny when you first started dating.

**Marriage Tip # 4**

Always kiss goodnight. Even if the argument is not over or the problem is not solved, make sure to kiss goodnight and say I love you! You never know when you'll no longer have the opportunity.

I'm not saying that these tips will work every time, there are certainly problems which need to be handled differently, but if you work hard at remembering why you love each other, you are bound to last! Forget about the rest, because the only thing that really matters is your love for each other!"

# CHAPTER III

## SIMPLE WAYS TO MAKE A MARRIAGE LAST

It takes work, patience and dedication to have a healthy marriage. There are things you can do to have a healthy marriage. Here are tips you can use to strengthen your marriage. These steps require real, committed effort on your part. Building a healthy marriage is not complicated or difficult if you're determined to follow basic principles. True love involves a giving—a sharing of plans, hopes and dreams between two people who want to build an entire life together until death does them part. They must be able to talk things over, smile into each other's eyes, share little joys and intimacies and stick together when the big trials come.

Trust each other, have a balance of power, enjoy each other, promote personal growth in each other, have a listening attitude, be consistently affectionate, use appreciative words, laugh frequently with each other and have a grateful heart.

### Be there

Your presence, both physical and emotional, is critical to the survival of your relationship. Try to be present in the moment and to be sensitive to your spouse's emotional state. Really listen when your spouse speaks. If your job or other obligations routinely keep you away from your spouse, take a hard look at your options and determine what is best for the overall health of your marriage.

### Be grateful

Before you rush to judge, take a step back and remember what you have in your partner. Is he or she loyal, considerate or kind? What flaws of yours does your spouse patiently endure?

## Be helpful

You shouldn't be helpful just for the sake of getting what you want. But you'd be surprised at how often helping your partner out—especially when he or she is stressed—can yield the kind of response you crave most. If you feel shortchanged on affection, communication or time, try being more helpful. It's not a magic formula guaranteed to bring results, but it can help improve your spouse's mood, and by extension, your relationship.

## Be forgiving

Be open. Make a decision to forgive your spouse. When images of a betrayal or hurt flash in your mind, think of a calming place or do something to distract yourself from dwelling on those thoughts. Don't throw an error or mistake back in your spouse's face at a later date. Don't use it as ammunition in an argument. Don't seek revenge or retribution. It will only extend the pain. Accept that you may never know the reason for the transgression. Remember that forgiveness doesn't mean you condone the hurtful behavior.

## Be sexually generous

Marriage is not an excuse to be a sexual slacker. Sexual incompatibility is listed as one of the top ten reasons for divorce in the U.S. Reproductive issues as well as sexual compatibility have led to separation and divorce. The problem can be amended by simply being openly honest with each other. When you put your spouse's sexual needs first, your own are likely to be satisfied as well. If for some reason your needs continue to be unmet, communicate with your spouse. Affirm your love for him or her while helping them understand what makes you feel loved. Some practice to affirm your love for him or her would be to do things together.

Infertility should not lead to divorce. Couples should seek professional help for these issues. There are options for the infertility problems with the advancement of science, new treatments are available. Another excellent option for childless couples would be adoption or foster parenting. Both are a blessing to the couples and the children.

## Be patient

Treat your spouse the way you want to be treated. Remember not everyone operates at the same speed. Those who get impatient quickly are usually those who operate at a faster speed. When it comes to your spouse, you just have to let them do things at their own speed. Even if that speed is very slow, you need to figure out a way to let go of the need to control how soon they get things done.

## Be adventurous

Some tools that an adventurer to a victorious marriage need are love and commitment, as well as hope or self-confidence through wise decision-making. Men and women who desire a marriage that last into eternity are challenged to make the adventure of their marriage, successful.

## Be committed

Marriage begins with commitment. Make a commitment to not accept thoughts contrary to your commitment to your spouse. "It's easy to be committed to your relationship when it's going well. As a relationship changes, I'm committed to this relationship, but it's not going very well—I need to have some resolve, make some sacrifices and take the steps I need to take to keep this relationship moving forward. I'm going to step up and take active steps to maintain this relationship, even if it means I'm not going to get my way in certain areas."

The following tips were excerpted from Seven Principles for Making Marriage Work, by John M. Gottman, Ph.D., and Nan Silver.

**Nurture Fondness and Admiration**

Two of the most crucial elements in a long-lasting romance are fondness and admiration. You must believe that your spouse is worthy of honor and respect. Remind yourself of your spouse's positive qualities and express out loud your fondness and admiration.

**Turn Toward Each Other**

In marriage people need their partner's attention, affection, humor and support. Turning toward each other is the basis of emotional connection, romance, passion, and a good sex life.

**Let Your Partner Influence You**

The marriages in which the husband treats his wife with respect and does not resist power sharing and decision making with her are the happiest, most stable ones. It's just as important for wives to treat their husbands with honor and respect. When the couple disagrees, these husbands actively search for common ground rather than insisting on getting their way.

Solve Your Solvable Problems. Start with good manners when tackling your solvable problems:

**Step 1**. Complain but don't criticize or attack your spouse. State your feelings without blame, and express a positive need (what you want, not what you do not want). Make statements that start with "I" instead of "you." Describe what is happening; do not evaluate or judge. Be clear. Be polite. Be appreciative. Do not store things up.

**Step 2**. Learn to make and receive repair attempts: De-escalate the tension and pull out of a downward cycle of negativity by asking for a break, sharing what you are feeling, apologizing, or expressing appreciation.

**Step 3**. Soothe yourself and each other: Conflict discussions can lead to "flooding." When this occurs, you feel overwhelmed both emotionally and physically, and you are too agitated to really hear what your spouse is saying. Take a break to soothe and distract yourself, and learn techniques to soothe your spouse.

**Step 4**. Compromise: Here's an exercise to try. Decide together on a solvable problem to tackle. Then separately draw two circles—a smaller one inside a larger one. In the inner circle list aspects of the problem you can't give in on. In the outer circle, list the aspects you can compromise about. Try to make the outer circle as large as possible and your inner circle as small as possible. Then come back and look for common bases for agreement.

### Overcome Gridlock

Perpetual conflicts that are gridlocked have a base of unexpressed dreams behind each person's stubborn position. In happy marriages, partners incorporate each other's goals into their concept of what their marriage is about. These goals can be as concrete as wanting to live in a certain kind of house or intangible, such as wanting to view life as a grand adventure. The bottom line in getting past gridlock is not necessarily to become a part of each other's dreams but to honor these dreams.

### Create Shared Meaning

Marriage can have an intentional sense of shared purpose, meaning, family values, and cultural legacy that forms a shared inner life. Each couple and each family creates its own micro culture with customs (like Sunday dinner out), rituals (like a celebration after the birth of a baby, birthday parties, vacations), and myths—the stories the couple tells themselves that explain their marriage. This culture incorporates both of their dreams, and it is flexible enough to change as husband and wife grow and develop. When a marriage has this shared sense of meaning, conflict is less intense and problems are unlikely to lead to gridlock.

Kindness looks to the core worth of another person and responds accordingly. Kindness doesn't mean <u>avoiding conflict</u> or even always "playing nice"—it just means processing through issues with a sincere respect for your spouse's feelings and humanity.

Dave Earley in <u>Secrets to a Better Marriage</u> lists Powerful Principles from the Bible. Earley writes, "God is the only one and true marriage expert. He has shared His knowledge with using the Bible. The foundation of your marriage will not be immediately noticeable, yet it is essential for the strength, growth, and quality of your marriage."

## Love When it is Difficult

The only person you can change is you. Change how you interact with that person who finds it difficult to love. Show them love in a variety of ways. Send cards, give home-baked goodies. Do household chores. Help however you can help. Do little and big things that show love. Be understanding of the discomfort or distrust that person may feel. Accept they may try to hurt you so you can be in the same pain they are. A person who finds love difficult is in pain somewhere in life, you can only change how you act and react to their pain. "The best gift you can give is the gift of genuine, undeniable, unconditional, sacrificial, selfless love."

Dr. Gary Smalley is a family counselor, president and founder of the Smalley Relationship Center and author of books on family relationships from a Christian perspective. In an interview, Gary Smalley was asked the question What are Love Skills? In his program, they teach three "love skills" that help a couple move into the fourth and fifth levels of intimacy. "The love skills act like an antibiotic killing divorce germs."

## The first love skill is the skill of honor.

It is the biggest antibiotic against divorce. Honoring is considering your mate more valuable than yourself. If a person communicates superiority to his or her mate, it can kill a marriage. John Gottman, Ph.D. calls this type of behavior contempt. Gottman says he can predict divorce with 100 percent accuracy if a person does not honor his or her mate." Smalley calls this type of behavior dishonor, a violation of Philippians 2. He teaches three steps in honoring a person.

First, says Smalley is to recognize your mate as valuable, important, and autographed by God.

Second, list all the things you treasure, admire, and appreciate about your mate, and review the list from time to time. Reviewing sets a rock-solid foundation to your marriage and gives you the energy to repair whatever is damaged after a conflict.

Show or express ways you appreciate your mate, without embarrassing him or her. For example, tell your children or friends how important your mate is to you. That's honor, the most important skill. In many cases, it's the only skill a couple needs. Honoring can also be applied to children and friends."

"Love, commitment, and faith are obviously important, but how well they argue determines whether a couple stays in love and has longevity in their marriage. Remembering that your mate's opinions, concerns, ideas, and thinking are more important than yours will help you argue with honor rather than with anger." This is why couples need to use the second love skill—which he calls the drive-through listening skill. This second love skill is based on James 1:19, 20.

> "My dear brothers and sisters, take note of this:
> Everyone should be quick to listen, slow to speak and
> slow to become angry, because human anger does not
> produce the righteousness that God desires."

"These drive-through listening skills are LUV—listening, understanding, and validating. This is similar to what happens at a drive-through restaurant. After you have placed your order, the employee repeats your order. You can then acknowledge whether the order is correct or not. In this second love skill, you first listen carefully to your mate. Next, to understand your mate, ask yourself, "What is my mate saying?" This may mean repeating what your spouse has said to clarify any misunderstanding. When you do this, you may be astonished by your mate's uniqueness.

The last step—validation—means you have understood your mate and you acknowledge his or her opinions as valuable, even if you do not agree. At this point the couple can begin to discuss solutions, determining what would benefit both of them."

The third skill is love-charging your mate's battery. According to Smalley you are to picture yourself as a battery with jumper cables. Symbolically attach them to your mate for 20 minutes a day at different times—a minute here, 2 minutes there, 30 seconds here—as you nurture or charge your mate's main-need battery. Some people have one or two predominant needs, and others have all seven of these needs. We have discovered that arguments in a marriage are the result of somebody's needs not being met, or they perceive that their needs won't be met. Arguments can cause the germs that infect or break up families. If I know my mate's needs, and God gives me the strength to understand and meet those needs, our arguments will be cut to almost nothing.

> Dr. Smalley states that there are seven needs that are important in marriages, especially pastoral marriages. They are:
>
> - A mutual commitment to maintain a vibrant relationship with Christ;
> - A mutual commitment to stay together and work at resolving conflicts;
> - The need to have verbal and physical tenderness from one's mate;
> - Connectedness—doing things together (a man's big need), or talking together (a woman's big need);
> - Agreement or inclusion in the decisions that affect both partners in a marriage;

- Acceptance of one spouse by the other for who he or she is and his or her thoughts, opinions, and feelings;
- The need to feel the other mate is being honest and trustworthy."

# CHAPTER IV

## KNOW EACH OTHER

"In order for a couple to work as a team, the partners have to know what each other is thinking," says Pauline Boss, Ph.D., professor of family social science at the University of Minnesota, and author of Family Stress Management. "When you and your spouse stop talking with each other, that's when marital problems escalate."

Understand Your Mate and Celebrate Your Differences: Men and women are different. The differences are what make the opposite sex so attractive—and so frustrating. The challenge of uniting two very different people is what drives us to God to see Him do the mysterious and glorious work of making us one. We need to appreciate each other's uniqueness if we hope to live together in harmony.

Pray for the ability to embrace, appreciate, and deal with you and your spouse's differences in healthy ways. Marriages are enhanced as we understand, appreciate, and use our differences to complement one another and draw close, not criticize each other and draw away. God has given wives and husbands different responsibilities. Husbands are to lead, love, train your children and provide for the family. (Ephesians 5, 1 Timothy 5:8)

Wives are to support husbands' leadership, respect, love your family and prioritize your family. (Ephesians 5, 1 Peter, Titus)

The sense of cooperation, the feeling that all are working together, talking together, laughing together is also of great value in the home. A person who does not fit easily in the home pattern and is a loner will carry this same quality into marriage. Those who are about to marry must fully realize that marriage demands that a husband and wife work together to make their marriage a successful one. One person alone cannot do it!

The true strength of family is seen when sorrow comes; death, illness, financial loss or the way they deal with the crisis. If they go to pieces and do not deal with the problem it is a foreshadow of how they will deal with sorrow and trials. The ability to laugh, a sense of humor makes life more enjoyable and livable.

## Background

You and your partner have different heredity, background and speak a different language. Heredity, environment, family, friends and education have formed you. In order to live with another person you need to know the various factors that went into making him as he is. Home is where he learns how to receive and give love; how to carry his share of the burdens of family life, to rejoice in the good things and not fall apart in trials and tribulations.

You can judge how your partner will treat you when you see how he treats his parents, his brothers and sisters and his friends. A sense of security, a feeling of self-confidence is needed by every mature person and only a mature person is capable of accepting the responsibilities of marriage. A person must feel needed and wanted. It is not enough to know in your mind but you must feel in your heart that you are needed and wanted. This feeling comes from the home.

Differences in priorities and expectations are listed as a cause for divorce. Though we try to harmonize our priorities, we still remain distinct and different individuals. The best solution is to meet halfway. Couples who encounter major differences in priorities regarding their lifestyle should sit down and try to come up with a compromise.

## Personality

You are two different individuals of different sexes and from different backgrounds who must unite to become one. It is important to understand that you are each unique in your own way. You must respect the individuality of the other and not try to change him or her to your own standard. Each is a person before he is a spouse. Each has his own temperament. The Greek father of medicine Hippocrates taught us that there are four temperaments. A temperament is part of your personality. Each temperament has good and bad inclination, the good to be developed and the bad to be controlled. Character is what you do with your temperament. You are not responsible for your temperament but you are responsible for your character. God gives you your free will and His grace, the necessary helps to develop a good character.

**Choleric**: The choleric's difficulty is that he drives himself too hard. In his efforts to reach his goal he often does not even notice the needs and feelings of others. In marriage a choleric man may drive himself so hard in his business that he has no time for his wife and family. A choleric woman may dominate her husband and become the very bossy and nagging type. Confidence and trust in themselves comes easily to the choleric; humility, sympathy and forgiveness come with difficulty.

**Sanguine**: A sanguine person is a happy warm, cheerful, outgoing person. A sanguine is optimistic and reacts greatly to praise and honors. On the negative side he is very restless and not a good sitter. At times the sanguine can be very flighty and irresponsible. A sanguine man can be a very good salesman because he likes to meet people. A sanguine wife may be a very poor housekeeper who is more interested in going than staying. She may be unable to spend money wisely.

**Melancholic**: A melancholic person is an introvert who finds himself more at home in his own internal world than in the external world of people and things. His emotions are deep and powerful. A melancholy husband or wife is very difficult to live with because they are subject to moods that start and stop without any apparent reason to the partner. The moody person pulls into his shell and will not let the partner follow. Such an individual finds it difficult to live with himself and others.

**Phlegmatic**: Such a person is usually an easy going person without the great show of emotions of the sanguine or the deep intensity of the emotions of the melancholic. A phlegmatic is usually in calm possession of himself and is not easily disturbed. He seems to be without fire in his decisions, emotions and actions. But he does have a great quality of stick-to-itiveness and does get there.

There are no pure temperaments; each individual has a mixture of several temperaments with one predominating. A husband and wife of different temperaments easily complement and fit together. Accept your own temperament and the temperament of your partner. Work with your good as well as with your bad qualities. Understand the other and help him gradually to develop his own good qualities and control the bad ones. Do not blame your bad actions on your temperament, but on your character which has not controlled the bad inclination of your temperament. Character must direct temperament. True understanding of self and the other leads to a very happy marriage.

## Education

Those with the same intellectual background have common interests and communicate easily and have a better chance for a happy marriage. Study the Bible and other sources to improve your marriage and attend Marriage Retreats, Seminars and Conferences together.

## Friends

"Tell me who your friends are and I will tell you who you are." Friends say a lot about your values and preferences. If you and your partner do not associate with friends you may become bored with each other. Try to become friends with your partner's friends, but keep some of your own. Never have a best friend of the opposite sex as many affairs begin by friendship and sharing the difficulties and weaknesses of one's partner.

## Explore Common Interests

Couples thrive when they share similar interests. That doesn't necessarily mean each partner will enjoy every activity, but it opens up the opportunity for greater sharing and compromise. Doing things separately is not bad; however, common interests are important to healthy marriages. A common interest may be cooking or eating new foods together, going for walks or playing cards. The goal is to have something outside of your family that you both enjoy.

## Look for the Best in Each Other

When you met your partner, you fell in love with some of his or her wonderful qualities. Over time, however, your view of those qualities may have changed. For example, he may have been really good at saving money when you met. Now you just think he's cheap! Give each other the benefit of the doubt and create a list of all the things you love about your partner. It will help you to fall in love all over again! The Apostle Paul commanded:

> "Husbands, love your wives and do not be harsh with them." (Colossians 3:19).

## Enhance Your Love Map

Emotionally intelligent couples are intimately familiar with each other's world. They have a richly detailed love map—they know the major events in each other's history, and they keep updating their information as their spouse's world changes. He could tell you how she's feeling about her boss. She knows that he fears being too much like his father and considers himself a "free spirit." They know each other's goals, worries, and hopes.

## Commitment and Trust

Marriage is a "test" to see how loyal you will be to your mate with whom you share this relationship and to God's instruction regarding marriage. How much will you "give" of yourself to this other human being? How much will you be patient, kind and humble in order to make it work? Additionally, "God despises the selfishness, the lust, the vanity, the self-centeredness and the "treachery" that is nearly always present when marriage is ruptured by divorce."

In the teaching of the Apostle Paul we read:

> "Wives, submit yourselves to your own husbands as you do to the Lord. For the husband is the head of the wife as Christ is the head of the church, his body, of which he is the Savior. Now as the church submits to Christ, so also wives should submit to their husbands in everything. Husbands, love your wives, just as Christ loved the church and gave himself up for her." (Ephesians 5:22–25)."

These verses clearly show that marriage is a type of the relationship between Christ and the Church. The relationship is one of total submission to one another and to the will of God. It is to be a relationship lasting "till death do us part." It is to picture the love, concern and the trust and stability that exist between Christ and His Church.

Successful marriage requires effort. You must both work at it putting thought and energy into building your marriage. Never take it for granted. Pray about your marriage. Make a mutual commitment to make your marriage last. This builds within your marriage a sense of "trust" and of stability.

King Solomon, the author of Proverbs wrote:

> "A wife of noble character who can find? She is worth far more than rubies. Her husband has full confidence in her and lacks nothing of value. She brings him good, not harm, all the days of her life." (Proverbs 31:10–12).

What a beautiful picture of loving service and commitment of a godly wife! Such a wife ought to be deeply appreciated and treasured. Her husband should certainly respond by loving, honoring, protecting, providing and serving her in every way he can. A decent husband should never, let his mind or his emotions get involved romantically with another woman. Jesus Christ calls this kind of lustful thinking adultery:

> "But I tell you that anyone who looks at a woman lustfully has already committed adultery with her in his heart." (Matthew 5:28).

If acted upon, such a treacherous deed will not only devastate his wife and probably wreck their marriage; it will bring about a depth of sorrow and agony—let alone anger to the spouses. The One who made us male and female tells us:

> "But a man who commits adultery has no sense; whoever does so destroys himself." (Proverbs 6:32).

Such selfish behavior will virtually "tear the heart" out of a loving spouse who finds that they have been defrauded and dishonored in this way. Certainly the same thing happens to a wife who finds herself defrauded. For the deep feelings of love and trust, of family and home, of deep commitment and security are suddenly shattered! No wonder this passage continues:

> "For jealousy is the rage of a man: therefore he will not spare in the day of vengeance. He will not regard any ransom; neither will he rest content, though thou givest many gifts." (vv. 34 35).

Make a profound commitment to honor your marriage vows in every way! We should study God's Word on this subject, pray daily regarding our marriage and our family, thank God regularly if we have a loving and faithful mate, and do all within our power—with God's help—to build a deep sense of love, of trust and of stability within our marriage.

"Enjoy life with your wife, whom you love, all the days of this meaningless life that God has given you under the sun—all your meaningless days. For this is your lot in life and in your toilsome labor under the sun." (Ecclesiastes 9:9).

In this physical life there is no greater blessing than this kind of sanctified relationship! To avoid boredom in marriage which can become much more noticeable and intolerable after longer years of marriage you should try to celebrate your marriage often. Remember the good things and the accomplishments that were previously made possible throughout your union. This can help shift the focus from the negatives to the positives. Try new things like traveling occasionally, eating out or planning long-term projects.

# CHAPTER V

## HOW TO COMMUNICATE IN YOUR MARRIAGE

"Communication Breakdown in relationships is the number two cause of divorce in the U.S. Communication is the key when it comes to relationships—and marriage is no exception. When communication problems start surfacing, it is a hint that your relationship is going downhill. Many couples often say "we just cannot communicate, or we just do not understand each other. While talking does resolve issues, ego clashes tend to keep this option at bay thus making communication breakdown one of the top reasons for divorce.

Statistics on divorce suggest that 67.5 percent of divorce cases have lack of communication in marriage as the driving factor." When communication breaks down, barriers build up, until the cold shoulder is the normative posture in a marriage. What you communicate, how you communicate and when you communicate is where we have to focus. We were created for communication, especially in marriage. "Of all places, marital communication should reflect the intimate and harmonious communication of God Himself.

For God is a Trinity—Father, Son, and Holy Spirit—the only true and perfect Communication from all eternity. Whatever intimate and harmonious communication is, it is found perfectly in the Trinity. And we were created in God's image. So we were created for communication, communication that is designed for beauty, intimacy, and harmony. Of all places, this should be best expressed in our Christian marriages."

Communication is the foundation of every good relationship, especially marriage. Too many times we are raised in homes where good communication skills just weren't made available, due to the fact that parents just didn't know how to communicate appropriately themselves. If you don't share your feelings and the reasons for your feelings, you are not communicating and without communication a marriage is bound to fail." Avoid exaggerations and absolutes: most, least, worst, bigger, "you always" and "you never."

Good communication is not always about agreement, but when you are in disagreement it most likely means that you are communicating well and clearly stating your position. Improve Your Communication Skills. Why do husbands and wives fail to communicate more fully with one another? Learn how to listen and when to talk. You should never assume your partner knows what you are thinking or feeling. Tell your spouse what is going on and, as a spouse, know when to simply listen. Learning to really hear your partner is a skill that may require practice.

There are many resources available like books, marriage education workshops and online courses. All these options can help couples learn how to communicate more effectively. Couples need to communicate in a positive way. Remember that "listening" to your mate's innermost hurts and concerns does not automatically call for your "judgment" or for your advice. Often it is better just to be someone to talk to. Then, over time, your mate will usually solicit your advice or comment. But let that be done on their initiative, not yours. But you need to show love and concern.

You need to be willing to take time to really "listen" to your mate—showing genuine interest in what your sweetheart is saying and is going through. In this process, learn to ask questions and draw your mate out so you can more fully understand the situation: "Tell me more!" "I see. Do I understand this is what you are saying?" "I hadn't realized that. Please help me understand more completely so I can share your concern," and similar words of loving concern. Communication is key for a powerful relationship.

Learn to respond to one another openly and lovingly. Have no improper secrets. Bear no grudges. This is your only life, your only mate, your only love. Learn to think and feel in unison, solving all your problems together as a team. The mutual encouragement and stimulation you will feel, along with the added warmth and love you will experience, will add an extra dimension of understanding and purpose and joy to your life that cannot be obtained in any other way. Remember that, in marriage you should try to keep communication positive. For one partner to be constantly "picking at" or criticizing the other is not the kind of communication we are talking about! This type of negative harping is destructive to a marriage and should be avoided at all costs.

A man should not be continually haranguing and correcting his wife! How can she respond to him as a loving sweetheart when she is regularly "put down" and corrected by her husband? And the Bible makes it very plain that a wife is equally wrong if she is continually complaining, griping or haranguing her husband."

> "Better to live on a corner of the roof than share a house with a quarrelsome wife." (Proverbs 21:9).

But, again, the loving, positive flow of communication, information and sharing of plans and dreams between a husband and wife is the very essence of a happy marriage. Think about it! Even God "shares" His hopes and plans with us!

> "I no longer call you servants, because a servant does not know his master's business. Instead, I have called you friends, for everything that I learned from my Father I have made known to you." (John 15:15).

If the living Jesus Christ was concerned enough to share "all things" with us that He heard from God the Father, how much more should we be willing to open up and share our thoughts and dreams with our own mates?

A husband worthy of the name ought to cultivate the habit of talking over plans and hopes with this wife, sharing with her many of his innermost thoughts and desires and make her feel deeply "a part" of him. This very attitude and approach means more to a woman than most men can even realize! In I Corinthians Chapter 13 shows love is an attitude more than an emotion. Yet very few husbands share their lives in this way with their mates. As the marriage continues and children come along, the wife's interest and talk is increasingly about her children and domestic details that usually hold little or no interest for the husband.

The couple often takes for granted each other's attitudes on certain topics rather than even bothering to discuss them. Most husbands care to hear only good news about their children, and are either irritated or bored if the wife confides in them the detailed problems involved in rearing their family. Wives usually miss their husbands most when the children are small. Having no adult in the house to talk to all day, such wives feel an urgent necessity to talk with their spouses at night. But many husbands retreat behind their papers or quietly turn on the television rather than endure what they feel is a boring repetition of household frustrations.

Never take advantage of your mate's honesty, openness or self-disclosure! He or she will close up like a clam in the future. Regard the communication you share in marriage as a sacred trust to be kept confidential just between the two of you. Never use as a "weapon" to gain advantage in an argument or any other situation.

The approach of praising and encouraging your mate is of vital importance. Be sure your praise is sincere and specific. Praising your wife for lovingly preparing a special meal, praising your husband for usually getting up first and warming up the car—these are examples of the kind of thoughtfulness and encouraging remarks that can inspire your mate and build love and appreciation within your marriage.

Make time for meaningful conversation. Know what is important to your partner and make time to talk about your shared goals (both short and long-term). Remind yourselves of the unique history you have together to share memories. Look through wedding and family photo albums together. Develop traditions and rituals that strengthen your marriage. Talking together about your future and your past can keep you bonded to one another. Examine these communication tools that will move your relationship forward and even make it stronger.

Who Is This Person? If it's your spouse, you owe this person. Don't you think they deserve your best effort at communication without sloppy, unprepared rants? The person walking with us through life deserves courtesy and a lot more. So before we attempt any kind of communication we should remind ourselves of this person's place and value in our life.

Well, what is communication? Would you agree that communication could be defined as simply sending a message to someone? We must first know what message we're trying to send. Thinking out loud, though understandable at times, should be prefaced and used only with extreme caution. You don't want to realize that what you're saying is selfish, insensitive, harsh, unreasonable or even incorrect after you've said them out loud to your spouse. Words are hard to take back and often leave hurt and doubt in the heart of your spouse.

Sensitive topics, it would be wise of you to say your words out loud to yourself first instead of "trying them out" on your spouse. You might have some editing to do on some of the words that come out wrong. You should work and be careful with your words. In a relationship you'll likely find that much hurt and damage could be avoided if we actually did some preparation before we attempted to communicate. Be kind and do your best to put yourself in the position of the listener. Think about the words before you say them so that you aren't unintentionally harsh or unclear.

When You Communicate: "When angry—it's best that you go to another room and listen to your words out loud before you say them to your spouse." It's also best to wait until you calm down. You are more reasonable and rational when you have your temper in control. We all face specific barriers that hinder a deepening communication in our marriages.

First, we all carry some baggage with us from our upbringing. Our parents may have never communicated with each other or with us. They may have told us that children are to be seen and not heard.

Second, we live in an isolating culture. Things like television, the

Internet, and video games isolate us from those nearest and dearest to us. (More in the chapter on Technology) We get comfortable finding our own meaning, purpose, and values without having to interact and communicate with others.

Third, we are bombarded with outside pressures.

Fourth, we tend to be lazy, gravitating to the nearest comfort zone. Real marital communication takes time, effort, and planning.

Fifth, we may be fearful of showing our emotions or of being rejected if we communicate openly and honestly

Marital Communication can be nurtured into the joy that God intended for couples. As a couple before God, commit yourselves to the recovery of a Trinitarian communication. Ask Him to nurture the language of intimacy and relationship in your lives. Great communication begins with God, the Author and Perfector of all communication.

> "The hearing ear and the seeing eye—the Lord has made both of them (Proverbs 20:12).

"Accept the fact that God alone is the perfect Communicator. Your marriage will always need His redeeming touch for intimate communication to develop. And you will never arrive at the place of perfect communication in marriage."

> "For the eyes of the Lord are upon the righteous (those who are upright and in right standing with God), and His ears are attentive to their prayer. But the face of the Lord is against those who practice evil [to oppose them, to frustrate, and defeat them]. (Psalms 34:15; 1 Peter 3:12).

"Recognize that there will be times of spontaneous communication as well as structured communication in your marriage. So be sensitive to both. Grab it when the need bursts into your marriage. Plan it when you are strung out on life's pressures."

Effective communication begins with discovering transparency. Transparency in marriage is described in Genesis before the fall:

"Adam and his wife were both naked, and they felt no shame." Genesis 2:25

They were without disguise or covering, without any mask. They were uncovered physically, and they did not cover up emotionally. Before the fall, Adam and Eve were a picture of true transparency—being real, open to each other, and unafraid of rejection. After the fall, we read,

"Then the eyes of both of them were opened, and they realized they were naked;" Genesis 3:7

The famous fig leaf aprons were only part of their cover-up. Sin introduced a lot more than modesty. It also brought deceit, lying, trickery, half-truths, manipulation, misrepresentation, distortion, hatred, jealousy, control, and many other vices, all causing us to wear masks.

Many people spend tremendous time and energy building facades to hide their insecurities. They are afraid that if someone finds out who they really are, they will be rejected. For many men in particular, deep and honest communication can be very threatening. Too many wives and husbands are afraid to be honest with each other. The Scriptures, however, emphasize being open and vulnerable. Paul modeled transparency when he wrote to the Corinthians, many of whom were not exactly his admirers:

"For I wrote you out of great distress and anguish of heart and with many tears, not to grieve you but to let you know the depth of my love for you." (2 Corinthians 2:4) Paul was not afraid to weep or say, "I love you." Jesus wept over the death of Lazarus (John 11:35) and lamented His rejection by hard-hearted Jerusalem (Luke 13:34).

Scripture warns about being too open and honest. Solomon wrote,

"Sin is not ended by multiplying words, but the prudent hold their tongues." (Proverbs 10:19).

Words can hurt. They cut, rip, and wound. As Solomon also said,

"A person is praised according to their prudence, and one with a warped mind is despised." (Proverbs 12:18).

If you're a spouse who uses words rashly, then you would do well to "hold your tongue." Many couples would improve their relationships if both partners would use words that are gentle and full of encouragement and praise. In marriage, partners need to affirm each other often. The Bible encourages deeper communication but cautions against using it recklessly. How can you tell the difference between what is appropriate and inappropriate?

Deep communication takes most of us a long time to achieve. You or your spouse may have come from a family where open communication was discouraged or even punished. It may take years to reach a deep, satisfying level of transparency, but every couple needs to be headed in the right direction. Just as you do when you learn and sharpen most skills, with communication you start at easier levels and work your way toward proficiency.

**The fifth**, or lowest, level of communication is cliché conversation, where you share nothing of substance with the other person: "Hello, how are you doing? Hot, isn't it? Have a nice day."

**The fourth**, conversation involves reporting the facts. You share what you know but little more than that. You expose nothing of yourself and are content to report what so-and-so said or what so-and-so did.

**The third**, you share your opinions—your ideas and judgments about things. You finally start to come out of your shell and reveal a little bit of who you are. You watch the other person carefully, and when you sense even the slightest question or rejection, you retreat.

**The second**—emotional sharing—what you feel. Here you must be careful to avoid hurting your spouse. But many marriages are in such need of sharing feelings that the risk must be taken. If you can't share

44

feelings with your spouse, your marriage is on superficial ground. You won't grow, and neither will your partner.

**The First Level**, communication requires a deep degree of trust, commitment, and friendship. Transparency—being completely open with the other person. Transparency means sharing the real you, from the heart. You reserve the transparency level for your spouse and perhaps a few others who are very close to you. Becoming transparent with many people can be dangerous. For example, sharing too much of whom you are with someone of the opposite sex can lead to an affair. When spouses reach the transparency level, they operate with oneness. One can kindly say to the other, "I think you're angry. Is there something bothering you?" And the other can answer, "I think you're right. Maybe what is making me so mad is what my boss said to me in that meeting yesterday"

Reaching this level of meaningful communication is not easy, but the rewards far outweigh the cost. We all long deeply to be heard and understood. The most natural place for this to occur is within the safe harbor of a healthy marriage. That "safe" harbor can be created and maintained only by a couple committed to each other. At its root, love is a commitment. In marriage, it's a covenant. 1 John 4:18 embodies the commitment that brings freedom:

> "There is no fear in love. But perfect love drives out
> fear, because fear has to do with punishment. The one
> who fears is not made perfect in love."

How we communicate is crucial. The words we say and our tone of voice can really set the mood for how the conflict gets resolved.

### Steps to Effective Communication

**Pray**—Ask God to lead us in how we should approach a certain situation that is bothering us.

**Approach Respectfully**

Even though you may be angry with your spouse, try and make an effort to approach him/her with love and respect. If you read 1 Cor. 13:4-7 we need to be patient with our spouses—patience and respect equals love. We can't expect to go through our marriage without having to face conflict. God made us different, both with faults and strengths, however we were made to help each other grow spiritually. Learning effective communication skills will certainly help your marriage grow.

Couples who want to have a good marriage must learn to stay engaged. Paul said, writing to the church in Ephesus,

> "Therefore each of you must put off falsehood and speak truthfully to your neighbor, for we are all members of one body. "In your anger do not sin: Do not let the sun go down while you are still angry, and do not give the devil a foothold." (Eph. 4:25-27).

The principle is to not allow avoidance to become a corrosive pattern in your marriage. Couples should build oneness and intimacy by speaking openly and honestly about important issues in their marriage. You may need to learn how to listen to the INTENTION of their heart or listen to what they may WANT to communicate to you, but for some reason can't. Both of you may need to build up your speaking/listening skills so you can help each other in this. If your spouse won't cooperate in this mission to help your marriage, then work to make this happen as best as you can.

Below are a few scriptures relating to this subject I hope you will prayerfully study, asking God to speak to your heart as to how to apply them to your life with your marital partner:

> "(My son, do not let wisdom and understanding out of your sight, preserve sound judgment and discretion; they will be life for you, an ornament to grace your neck. (your outer self). (Proverbs 3:21-22)
>
> you have been trapped by what you said, ensnared by

the words of your mouth. So do this, my son, to free yourself, since you have fallen into your neighbor's hands: Go—to the point of exhaustion—and give your neighbor no rest! Allow no sleep to your eyes, no slumber to your eyelids. Free yourself, like a gazelle from the hand of the hunter, like a bird from the snare of the fowler."(Proverbs 6:2-5)

Whoever heeds life-giving correction will be at home among the wise. (Proverbs 15:31)

How much better to get wisdom than gold, to get insight rather than silver! (Proverbs 16:16)

To answer before listening—that is folly and shame. (Proverbs 18:13)

The tongue has the power of life and death, and those who love it will eat its fruit. (Proverbs 18:21) [This could also be death of communication in a marriage if you aren't careful.]

A person's wisdom yields patience; it is to one's glory to overlook an offense. (Proverbs 19:11)

Those who guard their mouths and their tongues keep themselves from calamity. (Proverbs 21:23)

Like apples of gold in settings of silver is a ruling rightly given. (Proverbs 25:11)

Ask God to show you how to be a dispenser of grace rather than a vessel of criticism with your partner in marriage.

# CHAPTER VI

## CONFLICT RESOLUTION

Learn to Negotiate Conflict. Conflict is a normal part of a relationship. There is a point, however, when it can increase in intensity and become emotionally and sometimes physically unsafe. Dr. Harley, author of the book, *Love Busters*, attributes marital conflict as being created in two ways: "(1) Couples fail to make each other happy, or (2) couples make each other unhappy." Working out problems in a relationship starts with understanding what your issues are and how to discuss them. Learn to pick your battles. Learn that men and women view things differently. Sometimes you have to agree to disagree. Spouses' do not have to agree on everything. Do not let an argument go on for very long and never go to bed mad.

"Let each party express how they feel about the situation. Work to express your feelings without using "YOU" messages. For example instead of saying "I hate it when you treat me that way." say "When you say this I feel this way." Own your feelings.

Next each person needs to express what they will do to help resolve the issue. This isn't time to try and change the other person. One step towards progress is acceptable and both parties should strive to work towards keeping their promise on what they plan to do to help resolve the conflict.

Come up with a plan of action. Think of actions, or words you can say to help fulfill your promise on what you are going to do to resolve the conflict. The resolution should be win—win for each person."

Whether the hurts are caused intentionally or inadvertently, they still hurt. If these conflicts go unresolved, they harden into "bricks" that form an invisible "wall of resentment." Conflict is inevitable in marriage. But it doesn't have to harm your relationship; it can actually strengthen it. If you and your spouse respond to conflict in a healthy way, conflict will become the doorway to intimacy between you because it will deepen your understanding of each other.

Your spouse has an amazingly valuable and incredibly vulnerable heart, Ask God to show you what emotional buttons your spouse is pushing through the conflict and how that makes you feel. Also ask God to reveal how you're pushing your spouse's emotional buttons through the conflict. Then pray for the power you need to gain control over the conflict and use it to accomplish something constructive in your relationship.

Remove resentment and resolve conflicts. Do not let little things that bother you build up until one of you explodes the issue into a large fight. If you are angry about something and do not try to talk about it with your spouse within 48 hours, let it go. If your spouse does not want to discuss the matter, set an appointment within the next 24 hours to have the discussion. Do not bring in past history. No name calling allowed and no hitting below the belt. Keep it between the two of you. Do not bring a third party into the situation.

Listen to one another. Be open to asking for forgiveness and being willing to forgive. Even though it may be hard to forgive your spouse, not forgiving can cause more harm both emotionally and physically to yourself and to your marriage. Holding a grudge is letting someone else live in your head rent free. Show humility: I was wrong. Show sensitivity: I am sorry. Reconciliation: Please forgive me. Restoration: I forgive you and I love you. If you and your spouse have an area of conflict that you just can't resolve, consider enlisting a counselor.

Look in the Mirror. Is there distance in your relationship with your mate? Without accusing your mate, what problem can you own and admit?

Where have you been insensitive to your mate's feelings?

What do you need to ask forgiveness for?

What do you need to forgive?

Will you reaffirm your love?

Will you do your part to tear down any and all relational walls and pull out every relational weed?

## Learn to Fight Fair

Though conflict is inevitable, it does not have to be devastating. Successful conflict resolution has certain rules that make it instructive and constructive rather than destructive. Avoid exaggerations and absolutes: most, least, worst, biggest," you always," "you never"; derogatory or sarcastic labels or names: spoiled brat, nut, wimp, jerk, creep, prom queen, diva, big hero. Comparisons: "Sarah's husband always . . ." "Josh's wife would never . . ." Sideswipe words or indirect attacks: "Most husbands take out the trash . . . ." "Seventy five percent of the wives in America would agree with me . . ." Defensive attacking responses: "What about you?" "The only reason I ever do that is because you . . ." Manipulative threats: "If you do that again, I'm leaving . . ." "If that's the way you want it, I'll never again."

## Acknowledge that a problem exists.

Be careful to attack the problem and not the person. Admit your share of the problem and ask for forgiveness. Use the inevitable conflicts of life to draw closer to your mate, not further apart. Conflict is not the problem. All married couples have disagreements; it's not knowing how to effectively argue that creates difficulty in a marriage. Make the effort to be honest about conflict and approach it with self-control. Do not yell. Do not scream. Do not talk in a threatening tone. Work toward resolution and use conflict to build bridges, not walls. Be honest. Stay controlled. Seek resolution, not walls. Cancel bitterness, replace it with active love.

## 24 Guidelines for Resolving Conflicts in Marriage

These were excerpted by New Life Magazine from the following "7

Secrets of a Happy Family" by Dr. Paul Meier and Richard Meier. Disagreements are sure to happen in a marriage, but they do not have to lead to hurtful arguments. Here are some suggestions to help resolve conflicts with your spouse.

1. Sincerely commit your lives to Jesus Christ as Lord.

2. Consider the marriage a life-long commitment, just as Christ is eternally committed to His bride, the Church.

3. Agree to always listen to each other's feelings, even if you disagree with the appropriateness of those feelings.

4. Commit yourselves to both honesty and acceptance.

5. Determine to attempt to love each other unconditionally, with each partner assuming 100 percent of the responsibility for resolving marital conflicts (the 50/50 concept seldom works).

6. Consider all the factors in a conflict before bringing it up with your mate.

7. Confess any personal sin in the conflict to Christ before confronting your mate.

8. Limit the conflict to the here and now—never bring up past failures, since all past failures should have already been forgiven.

9. Eliminate the following phrases from your vocabulary:
    a. "You never" or "You always"
    b. "I can't" (always substitute "I won't")
    c. "I'll try" (usually means "I'll make a half-hearted effort but won't quite succeed")
    d. "You should" or "You shouldn't" (these are parent-to-child statements).

10. Limit the discussion to the one issue that is the center of the conflict.

11. Focus on that issue rather than attacking each other.

12. Ask your mate if he would like some time to think about the conflict before discussing it (but never put it off past bedtime—see Eph. 4:26).

13. Each mate should use "I feel . . ." messages, expressing his response to whatever words or behavior aroused the conflict. For example, "I feel angry toward you for coming home late for supper without calling me first" is an adult-to-adult message, whereas "You should always call me when you're going to be late for supper" is a parent-to-child message. A parent-to-child message will cause the mate to become defensive.

14. Never say anything derogatory about your mate's personality. Proverbs 11:12 tells us that, "He who belittles and despises his neighbor lacks sense, but a man of understanding keeps silent."

15. Even though your mate won't always be correct, consider your mate an instrument of God, working in your life. Proverbs 12:1 says, Whoever loves instruction and correction loves knowledge, but he who hates reproof is like a brute beast, stupid and indiscriminating.

16. Never counterattack, even if your mate does not follow these guidelines.

17. Don't tell your mate why you think he or she does what he does (unless he asks you), but rather stick to how you feel about what he does.

18. Don't try to read your mate's mind. If you're not sure what he meant by something he said, ask him to clarify it.

19. Commit yourselves to follow the instructions in dealing with anger Biblically. This will help you avoid depression, which results in increased irritability and increased marital conflicts.

20. Be honest about your true emotions, but keep them

under control. Proverbs 29:11 says, " Fools give full vent to their rage, but the wise bring calm in the end."

Proverbs 15:18 "A hot-tempered person stirs up conflict, but the one who is patient calms a quarrel."

21. Remember that the resolution of the conflict is what is important, not who wins or loses. If the conflict is resolved, you both win. You're on the same team, not opposing, competing teams.

22. Agree with each other on what topics are "out of bounds" because they are too hurtful or have already been discussed (for example, in-laws, continued obesity, and so on).

23. Pray about each conflict before discussing it with your mate.

24. Commit yourselves to carefully learn and practice these 24 guidelines for "fighting fair" in marriage and agree with each other to call "foul" whenever one of you accidentally or purposefully breaks one of these guidelines. (You may choose to agree on a dollar fine for each violation!)

Dr. Willard Harley, has created three promises for couples to make when they exchange rings. These promises embody what a husband and wife should expect of each other.

**The first is the promise of care**: I promise to meet your most important emotional needs. Try to identify your own needs prior to marriage and then promise to meet each other's needs after you are married.

**The second is the promise of time**: I promise to give you my undivided attention at least 15 hours each week. Time should be set aside to meet each other's important emotional needs of affection, sexual fulfillment, conversation, and recreational companionship.

**The third is the promise of protection**: I promise to avoid being the cause of your unhappiness. Avoid the Love Busters—selfish demands, disrespectful judgments, angry outbursts, dishonesty, annoying habits, and independent behavior. Also avoid the things that can ruin a marriage listed in the following chapter.

# CHAPTER VII

## HABITS THAT DESTROY ROMANTIC LOVE

### Behaviors That Can Ruin Your Marriage

Willard F. Harley, Jr. describes destructive habits as "Love Busters." He lists in his book by the same title "Love Busters";

**"Selfish demands** (who wants to live with a dictator),
**Disrespectful judgments** (Who wants to live with a critic),
**Angry outbursts** (Who wants to live with a time bomb)
**Dishonesty** (who wants to live with a liar),
**Annoying habits** (Who wants to live with a dripping faucet), and
**Independent behavior** (Who wants to live with an inconsiderate jerk)".

I have found many more destructive habits and the most prominent causes of divorce. Identifying the major causes of divorce will prevent us from falling into these areas. Do men and women expect a lot from each other? When one of them or both can't fulfill the partner's expectations the marriage may be at stake. What are the things that could hurt the marriage? "There are more than 30 million happy couples in America; more than 60 million people in the United States are happily married. The Bible says, God hates divorce. So be on your guard, and work for your marriage.

> "The man who hates and divorces his wife," says the
> LORD, the God of Israel, "does violence to the one he
> should protect," says the LORD Almighty.(Mal.2:16)

The best way to avoid divorce then, is by avoiding the situations that lead to it. Most of these situations are influenced by factors such as age, religion, education, financial condition and norms of the society. We need to strengthen our marriage around the Word of God.

"Roughly 20 million American children under 18 years of age in the United States live with just one parent. This represents 28 percent of all children. The majority of these or 84 percent—live with their mother. In other words, approximately 17 million American children live in fatherless homes!" We have produced an entire generation of young people seemingly unafraid to do wrong, who are blatant in their sarcasm and in their rebellion against the rules of society and against the laws of God, the "in your face" generation. In a prophecy that certainly refers to our day, the prophet Isaiah wrote:

> "I will make mere youths their officials; children will rule over them." People will oppress each other—man against man, neighbor against neighbor. The young will rise up against the old, the nobody against the honored." (Isaiah 3:4–5).

We need to take a serious look at the causes of divorce and take a proactive stance. We need to do more counseling of the youth before they even get into a relationship. Marriage is the most blissful thing in the world. The goal of marriage is to have a union for life; an intellectual, social, spiritual, emotional and physical union. A happy marriage can make your life a "Heaven". We need to practice prevention rather than correction after the fact.

"When most couples first marry, they forget to take into account the other person's feelings. They have been so lovey-dovey during the courtship and engagement; that they assume the feelings, thoughts, needs, and wants they have are the same as their spouses. Marriage is when all of the stuff that was hiding under the covers starts to come out." These are the little things that the enemy uses to get a foothold in your marriage; he uses the culture we live in today. God does not want us to be molded by the culture. In Romans 12:2 we read:

"Do not conform to the pattern of this world, but be
transformed by the renewing of your mind. Then you
will be able to test and approve what God's will is—
His good, pleasing and perfect will."

God wants us to let Him form us, not the world. Many married
couples decide not to have children because no one wants to stop their
career for children. Couples bring many differences into their
marriage and they must work to reach oneness. Satan attacks the
differences in values, vocations, denominations, finances and
families. Don't get hung up on the differences, but instead discuss
them and come to a happy medium. Your spouse is only human and
can't meet all of your expectations. Have expectations in your
marriage for God. He can handle it because He knows you intimately.
Delight in your spouse. It's about enjoying your mate in your
differences and celebrating them.

The best place to start would be by not practicing the things that
could ruin your marriage. The following is a list of behaviors or habits
that can ruin a marriage. The breakdown of marriage is legendary. The
statistics are terrible. "Associated Press recently reported that some
19.4 million American adults are currently divorced, representing 9.8
percent of the population. " So nearly one out of ten American adults
is now divorced! Of course, many others were previously divorced
but have since remarried. By any estimate, tens of millions of
Americans have at one time or another gone through the trauma of
divorce and other tens of millions have been deeply hurt by divorce:
children, close relatives, friends and associates.

It is sad to say, but divorce is "as American as apple pie!"
Negative behavior patterns can destroy a relationship. Remember, just
about everything that you and your spouse do affects the feeling of
love you have for each other. How spouses affect each other has a
tremendous bearing on the success and failure of marriage.

**We will begin with:**

## Infidelity

There is no good excuse for infidelity. Women forgive infidelity more easily than men. Married partners need to have self-control and should not give into temptations.

## Dishonesty

Dishonesty in relationships exists when one party withholds or alters facts about themselves or a situation and presents it as truth. Dishonesty hinders intimacy between the parties and eliminates the validity of the relationship.

## Intolerance

Perfection? None of us are perfect. We want our partners to change but we don't want to change. Intolerance by either partner can hurt the marriage. Angry outbursts are many times the result of intolerance and they also hurt relationships.

## Escalation

"According to the researchers, "escalation occurs when partners respond back and forth negatively to each other, continually upping the ante so the conversation gets more and more hostile." 1 Peter 3:9 says,

> "Do not repay evil with evil or insult with insult. On the contrary, repay evil with blessing, because to this you were called so that you may inherit a blessing."

But this is exactly what happens with escalation. Each negative comment increases the level of anger and frustration, and soon a small disagreement blows up into a major fight." Once negative comments are made, they are hard to take back and drive a knife into the partner's heart. Proverbs 12:18 says,

> "The words of the reckless pierce like swords, but the tongue of the wise brings healing."

## Invalidation

Invalidation is a pattern in which one partner subtly or directly puts down the thoughts, feelings, or character of the other." Invalidation can be caustic, in which one partner (or both) attacks the other person verbally. You can hear, and even feel, the contempt one partner has for another. Sarcastic phrases like "Well, I'm sorry I'm not perfect like you "can cut like a knife. These are attacks on the person's character and personality that easily destroy a marriage.

Research has found that invalidation is one of the best predictors of future problems and divorce. A husband may invalidate a wife's fears about the safety of the children. A wife may invalidate a husband's desire to succeed in the company. Ultimately the partner receiving invalidating comments begins to share less and the intimate level of sharing evaporates. Oneness is lost.

## Abuse

Marital abuse from either the husband or the wife comes in different forms. They include things like telling a spouse that they are unwanted, name calling, ignoring the spouse, restricting the person to a room or emotional terrorizing or monitoring phone calls. Verbal insults, humiliation, taunts as well as intimidation—all of which combine to form severe emotional abuse, have a significant share in the total number of divorce cases in the United States.

## Physical Abuse

In some cases, it doesn't just stop at emotional abuse—but take a much violent way in form of physical abuse, such as beatings. Such abusive relationships have a significant share when it comes to reasons for divorce in America today. Verbal, emotional or physical abuse can ruin the marriage.

## Disrespectful Judgments

If a partner doesn't treat the other with respect, the marriage will be at risk. This is also a form of abuse. "A disrespectful judgment occurs whenever one spouse tries to impose a system of values and beliefs on the other. When a husband tries to force his point of view on his wife, he's just asking for trouble. When a wife assumes that her own views are right and her husband is woefully misguided—and tells him so—she enters a minefield." Spouses are known to use disrespectful judgments to get their needs met.

### Physical Incompatibility

One of the most common reasons for divorce is physical incompatibility between the couple; differences in needs, in sexual desires and lack of attraction that can be attributed—from loss of interest in partner to hectic lifestyle. The end result is nothing but disaster in form of divorce.

### Lack of trust

Trust by both parties is very important in a relationship. If one doesn't have faith in the other, the relationship will not work.

### Sex life

Sex plays an important vital role in any relationship. Apostle Paul writes in 1 Corinthians 7:5

> "Do not deprive each other except perhaps by mutual consent and for a time, so that you may devote yourselves to prayer. Then come together again so that Satan will not tempt you because of your lack of self-control."

If your sex life is not fulfilling, the relationship may fail. If your spouse has an emotional need, sex for example, you're obligated to devote time to meeting it. "Improper attitudes about sex, and not physical causes, bring couples to the breaking point. Both those who regard sex as being acceptable outside of marriage, as well as those who think of sex as dirty and wrong within marriage, are equally guilty of maintaining attitudes which are destined to cause serious trouble to any family relationship."

## Lack of Care

If a partner doesn't care about the other, the relationship will disintegrate. Promise to avoid being the cause of your spouse's unhappiness. Withdrawal and avoidance are two different manifestations of the problem wherein a partner is unwilling to get in or stay in a discussion that is too threatening.

## Withdrawal

Withdrawal can be as obvious as getting up and leaving the room or as subtle as 'turning off' or 'shutting down' during an argument. The withdrawer often tends to get quiet during an argument, look away, or agree quickly to a partner's suggestion just to end the conversation, with no real intention of following through."

## Avoidance

Avoidance reflects the same reluctance to get into certain discussions, with more emphasis on the attempt to not let the conversation happen in the first place. A person prone to avoidance would prefer that the topic not come up and, if it does, may manifest the signs of withdrawal just described."

Couples who want to have a good marriage must learn to stay engaged. Paul said, writing to the church in Ephesus,

> "Therefore each of you must put off falsehood and speak truthfully to your neighbor, for we are all members of one body. In your anger do not sin: Do not let the sun go down while you are still angry, and do not give the devil a foothold." (Eph. 4:25-27).

Although the immediate context in this passage is anger, the broader principle is the importance of not allowing avoidance to become a corrosive pattern in your marriage. Couples should build oneness and intimacy by speaking openly and honestly about important issues in their marriage.

## Financial problems

Financial problems can also affect marriages. "You need to consider the feelings of both spouses." Economic strain is something that all married couples are subjected to at some point in their life. Ensure that there are no serious financial problems in the family. Insufficient funds to cover debts cause increased arguments. The spender and the tightwad must have a budget to avoid serious problems. The Bible says

> "For the love of money is a root of all kinds of evil. Some people, eager for money, have wandered from the faith and pierced themselves with many grief's." (I Tim. 6:10)

## Concern about family

When a couple marries they become a family but eventually they also need to deal with their extended family and parenting issues. Both the partners should be concerned about the family and work together to make it strong.

## Criticism

Criticism can also hurt a marriage. According to Dr. John Gottman in his book, "The Seven Principles for Making Marriage Work" there are four horsemen of the Apocalypse that attack marriages. By attacking the personality or character of the other you damage the relationship. Criticism is one of those horses. Avoid using words such as 'you never', 'you always' 'you are' etc. There are various forms of criticism; joking, faultfinding, zingers and invalidating words.

## Addictions:

Marriages, families, and drug and alcohol abuse do not mix well. The abuse or use of alcohol or drugs (even prescription drugs) can hurt the marriage. Addicts do not only have degrading effects on their own self-image and their spouses, but they also leave disastrous emotional scars on their children, close relatives and friends. Being addicted to alcohol, cigarettes, drugs etc. is not just harmful for you, but for your marriage as well. There are many programs available to help overcome these addictions. Some of the steps with addiction help can include identifying the source of addiction, being honest about it and immediately seeking professional counseling intervention. In the United States addiction is one of the most draining causes and one of the top ten reasons for divorce.

## Annoying Habits

Here are some examples: Putting your feet on the furniture, laughing shrilly, taking forever to get to the point in a conversation, making embarrassing, humiliating, or degrading remarks about your spouse in public or engaging in childish bickering in public; responding in baby talk, flirting with other people of the opposite sex, nagging, being bossy.

## Immaturity

It is possible for a husband to be so self-centered that he doesn't care about the feelings of his wife (and that can be true of wives as well). It's sad that many young women (when they're dating) don't realize that a young man who doesn't care about anyone's feelings but his own probably won't care about her feelings either once they're married. It is possible for married adults to be as ungrateful as a small child. Many husbands and wives hardly know what it is to say, "Thank you." Often the words are absent because the feeling is absent.

There are husbands and wives locked in a constant battle to see who gets his way. It becomes a constant cycle of manipulative tricks, dramatic actions and reactions, sulking and shouting. Married life is for adults, not for children. Immaturity is the fourth leading cause of broken homes. There is an age when we are not sure about anything. (Adolescence) and marriage should be after this stage has passed.

## Jealousy

Wives often struggle with strong feelings of jealousy when they see their husbands talking to other women. Husbands can also feel a bought of jealousy when they see their wives paying too much attention to other men. Jealousy left unchecked can arouse fury and lead to destructive behavior. If one finds himself caught in the clutches of this weakness, he needs to concentrate on self-improvement, and should seek help.

## Irresponsibility

An irresponsible young man unwilling to work before marriage, the chances are that he'll continue the same behavior after marriage. The young lady who has shown no sense of personal responsibility before marriage will likely be unwilling in containing the home after marriage. Where there is love, one only thinks of the other therefore takes full responsibility to make his marriage work. Because of love, both husband and wife will then understand their respective roles and help each other fulfill it.

Marriage means responsibility. Love does not delegate everything to the other but there is reciprocity between the spouses. Love even extends one's responsibility outward. It extends a helping hand. Love makes one accountable to the other. Love not only makes them responsible spouses but even makes them responsible parents. Let responsibility not be a chore but a joy because it is an expression of love. It has that sense of ownership where both spouse now feel, "I have a family to take care of." Responsibility is key to a successful marriage because it is a result of love. Marriage means responsibility. And one can feel the joy of being a fulfilled spouse and parent.

## Communication Breakdown

Communication breakdown or as Dr. Gottman labels it: "Stonewalling". The companionship and completeness God intended for marriage grow out of communication as two people share each day the meaning of their lives. It is a hint that your relationship is going downhill when communication problems surface. While talking does resolve issues, ego clashes make communication breakdown one of the top reasons for divorce. People who stonewall simply refuse to respond. When you stonewall on a regular basis, you are pulling yourself out of the marriage, rather than working out your problems. Men tend to engage in stonewalling much more often than women do.

## Loss of Interest

Many people wrongly interpret loss of interest to physical intimacy. The fact is that it is more often related to the emotional aspect as compared to physical aspect of a relationship. The decrease in Physical Intimacy can be attributed to some things like stress outside the marriage, and medical reasons (like a lowered production of certain hormones) can cause this condition to come about. On the other hand, if this physical need is being met outside the marriage, there may a noticeable decrease in interest in this area when you are with each other.

## Shift in Priorities

"With time priorities change and your professional life becomes more important than the marriage. This and the lack of understanding between partners sound the death knell for their marriage."

## Independent Behavior

I define Independent Behavior as the conduct of one spouse that ignores the feelings and interest of the other spouse. Independent behavior is a problem in most marriages because we are all tempted to do whatever makes us happy, even when it makes our spouse unhappy (the Taker's rule). A Christian marriage involves more than the blending of two people. It also includes a third person—Jesus Christ—who gives meaning, guidance and direction to the relationship. When He presides in a marriage, then and only then it is a Christian Marriage.

**Relationships with in-law's:**

> "That is why a man leaves his father and mother and is united to his wife, and they become one flesh."(Genesis 2:24.)

Every couple should establish their own home away from parents. Problems will arise; differences will sometimes seem impossible and may cause conflict with the interests of spouse. According to a newly released study, men who are on good terms with their wives' parents are more likely to enjoy a long-lasting marriage than those who struggle to get along with their in-laws.

The following is a list of don'ts; behaviors that should not be practiced.

- **Don't over-romanticize**. Drop your delusions and see how much room it frees up for real love.
- **Don't overdramatize.** Some people thrive on drama. If you are one of those people, you are bound to be disappointed by any healthy relationship. Where no drama exists, drama-addicts will find ways to provoke or manufacture it.
- **Don't Procrastinate.** "One of the most crucial areas procrastination can affect is your marriage. Procrastination can affect your personal relationships. Not only does your spouse have to pick up the slack for responsibilities you no longer have time for, he/she will start to feel less like part of a team and more like a solo artist. This ongoing shift in the relationship can cause resentment and anger in your partner and lead to many problems.

Procrastination has a large effect on your personality by lowering your self-esteem, raising your anxiety levels and often leading to depression. All of these symptoms can be detrimental to how you deal with others—especially those closest to you. Procrastination, when perpetuated with the knowledge that it imposes undue hardships and problems upon your unfortunate partners, is a selfish, irresponsible, and disrespectful behavior of individuals who are deceptively nice during their courtship."

- **Don't nag or nitpick.** You may think your "constructive" criticism or helpful reminders will help mold your spouse into your idealized man or woman. More likely, it will just wear them out. You may or may not get what you want . . . and you are likely to get something you didn't want: resentment.

- **Don't lose focus.** We live in a hyper-saturated, hyper-stimulated world. Beauty is distorted, augmented and airbrushed. Willing sexual partners are around every dance club corner. Destructive behaviors are exaggerated (and glamorized) by "reality" shows. It seems like everyone is misbehaving and if you aren't, you must be missing out. But the desire for meaningful relationships is at the core of the human heart. You can try to take the shortcut to this kind of happiness by responding to every enticement that comes your way. Or you can choose to focus on a real relationship, and enjoy the enduring pleasures such a relationship provides.

- **Don't be selfish.** It sounds simple enough. But selfishness underlies most of our broken relationships—and it is a hard habit to break. Selfishness can take many forms: financial, behavioral, emotional or sexual. We all fall victim to selfishness from time to time, but chronic selfishness can do lasting damage to a relationship. Selfishness presents itself as a way to secure your own happiness, but most of the time, it actually erodes it.

Each of these risk factors can build barriers in a marriage leading ultimately to loneliness and isolation. All couples will engage in these types of behaviors at some point in their marriage, but when these behaviors become regular, the relationship has a high likelihood of failing. The research shows that couples that want a good marriage need to eliminate these risk factors from their marriage, or else the negative factors will overwhelm the positive aspects of the marriage. It is never too late to put your marriage back on track. If your marriage is filled with these issues, take notice, change yourself, work together and make improvements. If not, it could open the door for infidelity to occur and divorce is often inevitable.

# CHAPTER VIII

## AFFAIR PROOF YOUR MARRIAGE

### Infidelity

Infidelity is one of the most serious issues when it comes to disruption of marriage life, infidelity has a significant role to play in a large number of divorce cases in the U.S. While this reason has been there since quite a long time, the fact that it has combined with various other reasons today has made it all the more severe. "Jesus told parables about landowners who planted vineyards and protected them with hedges. When those hedges were trampled or removed, ruin came to the precious possessions of the landowners. Similarly we need to plant hedges around our marriages in order to protect them."

**Erect hedges to adultery**. In Proverbs 5:1 we are told

> "My son, pay attention to my wisdom, turn your ear to my words of insight, that you may maintain discretion and your lips may preserve knowledge. For the lips of the adulterous woman drip honey, and her speech is smoother than oil; but in the end she is bitter as gall, sharp as a double-edged sword. Her feet go down to death; her steps lead straight to the grave."

### Never be alone with a person of the opposite sex.

Always wear your ring. Always build your mate and marriage in public. Never share personal emotional feelings with any person of the opposite sex (other than your spouse). Be careful how you dress and how you touch or talk to persons of the opposite sex. Generally men respond to looks and women respond to words and to touch. If any of a spouse's basic emotional needs is not met, that spouse becomes vulnerable to the temptation of an affair. The most important need for women is affection and the most important need for men is sex. Adultery is never the right thing to do. It is always a sin. It is a sin against society, against marriage, against your children, and against your mate. Adultery is a sin against yourself. Most important it is a sin against God.

### Affairs don't only happen for sex.

Brad Lewis, writer for Focus on the Family wrote in his article "Why Affairs Happen" some reasons people get trapped in an affair:

### Failed Expectations.

Everybody gets into a relationship with some expectations—unfulfilled expectations cause unhappiness. This is yet another common reason for divorce in the U.S. Do not expect to change her or him. If you're planning to make changes in your partner, it is very likely that you're in for a sad disappointment.

Regardless of how sincerely one may promise to change after marriage, it is very unlikely that a person will suddenly alter the habits of a lifetime. When you hold to the belief that your marriage will last, it affects your approach to an imperfect spouse to your differences and conflicts and to your future together. Remember that you know your spouse's good and bad qualities; while you may only see someone else's good side because you don't know him or her well enough to see faults yet. That's known as "romanticizing" a relationship.

### To give a conscious or subconscious "wake-up call" to the spouse.

This might happen if your spouse has a different kind of "lover" outside of your marriage, such as a consuming career or hobby.

### To inflate a bruised ego.

You might want to get back at your spouse for something he or she did that hurt you rather than offering forgiveness and dealing with the root issue. "Looking for ego boosts outside your marriage. Men tend to turn to extramarital liaisons to build up their self-image or sexual self-esteem. Women are suspect to affairs to satisfy their longing for love, appreciation and tenderness. Beware of leaning on others beyond your marriage as primary sources for love, value and respect.

### A friendship gets out of control.

Whether or not you think it's healthy to have friendships with members of the opposite sex, take extra care in those relationships. Beth J. Leuders, also a writer for Focus on the Family has listed the following factors that can lead to marital unfaithfulness:

### Neglecting to talk openly with each other.

If you only talk to your spouse about the bills and household chores, you may be sliding into trouble. Holding in your thoughts and feelings does not enhance transparency in your relationship. Practice the art of small talk that can open the door to deeper sharing.

### Resisting conflict resolution.

Every couple runs into communication rough spots. It's important not to build walls between you and your spouse. Some people mask their hurt while others spew their emotions. Neither method is constructive. Both ways create relational roadblocks. Unresolved conflict leads to isolation and leaves you vulnerable to fleeing your marriage. Practice the steps listed in Chapter VI on Conflict Resolution.

### Discounting fun and relaxation together.

Think of the last time you and your spouse enjoyed a date or a weekend getaway together. As the old adage says, "Couples that play together, stay together." If career, family and homes responsibilities are crowding out laughter and friendship with your spouse, you need to book in some recreational retreats with each other.

### Increasing the time you spend apart.

The demands of work, travel, ill children or differing interests and hobbies are common issues that can keep couples apart. The more time you spend away from your spouse, the greater temptation to drift in your relationship.

### Allowing daily stresses and fatigue to sabotage your intimacy.

Packed schedules and raising children are two common reasons husbands and wives feel ho-hum in their relational intimacy. Romance, in an instant, can remind you of the reasons you love each other. All marriages require times of refreshing and an in-depth look at intimacy saboteurs.

### Letting your love life fizzle instead of sizzle.

Familiarity and boredom can creep into any marriage. Beware of shaking things up in your sex life by dumping your spouse for another more promising lover. If you or your partner suddenly is disinterested in sex with each other, be sure to explore the true reasons.

### Giving in to predictability.

A little mystery can go a long way in adding spice to your marriage. Many couples succumb to affairs out of fading interest in their spouses. One way to continue your wedded bliss is to surprise your mate with love notes or an occasional unexpected outing or gift.

### Living in denial.

Pretending that problems do not exist in your marriage will only widen the gap between you and your spouse. Many extramarital affairs start when a frustrated spouse searches for a reality check in marriage by turning to an officemate or friend of the opposite sex for support. Dare to face the truth of your marital struggles.

**Forgetting your commitment to each other.**

Over time couples are prone to forget why they fell in love. In our easy-come-easy-go culture, it takes courage and determination to honor commitment instead of convenience.

**Failing to resist come-ons and temptations.**

In our over-sexed world, even the most innocent husband or wife can fall prey to sexual temptations. Before you or your mate find yourself in compromising situations, talk about safeguards for your marriage. You may need to avoid after-work parties, certain hotels on business trips and sexually compromising magazines, movies or television shows. Thinking "Just this once," can lead to a lifetime of regret.

The following are three signs that should indicate to a person that they have crossed a marital boundary and may be dangerously close to having an affair.

**Emotional intimacy**

Do you find yourself sharing deep thoughts and feelings with a member of the opposite sex? Do you discuss details of your marriage and problems? Would you not want your spouse to hear what you are saying?

**Sexual tension**

Do you find yourself sexually attracted to another person and imagine being with that person in a romantic way?

**Secrecy**

Do you leave out details of your day because they include spending time with the person you are attracted to? Do you lie to your spouse about this person? Be honest with yourself and your spouse and do not ignore these signs.

It is a common myth that only people who are living in an unhappy marriage engage in affairs. This is far from reality. Sometimes, even people in happy marriages can find themselves tempted to become involved with another person outside of the marriage. The best way to prevent infidelity is to mutually "affair proof" your marriage.

## Steps to Prevent infidelity

### Keep up your physical appearance.

Whatever it took to attract your spouse to you, continue. Don't you think if your husband/wife liked your beautiful hair and the way you kept it nice before you were married, that they would expect you to keep it nice after you are married? If your breath was always sweet and nails/toenails done before you were married I would say it is reasonable to expect them to be done afterward. Take the time to always listen to and hear your spouse. Never be too busy or preoccupied to stop and hear the spirit of what they are saying. Always notice and take time to encourage your spouse. Words of affirmation go a long, long way.

### Make love often.

One of God's secrets to a great marriage is making love and seasoned intimacy. Having a good sex life and enjoying a sense of romance is an important part of a good marriage. Learn what each other's idea of romance is and discuss what feels romantic to you. Be imaginative and creative. Let your partner know how attractive they are to you. Having a mutually satisfying physical relationship strengthens and deepens the bond between you and your spouse. Pray for each other with each other every day. This binds your hearts and minds together. I realize that all of this works if both parties are sincere. If somebody is perpetrating, If someone is playing head games of course it won't work. But if you have two people who are sold out to God and yielding to one another with all their hearts, there is nothing God won't do for and through you.

**Don't ever talk to someone of the opposite sex about your personal and intimate business** or any business as a matter of fact that your spouse doesn't know about. Make your relationship with your spouse private and off limits to anyone else.

These are but a few of the safe guards you can take to prevent infidelity. Always be true to yourself and certainly to your spouse, it pays great dividends and makes for a beautiful marriage.

### How to Deal With Infidelity

Infidelity is breaking the trust of marriage. The trust is the unspoken vow that the couple will remain sexually exclusive. There is a certain level of emotional intimacy that is reserved for each other not to be shared with others. Infidelity occurs when one partner in the relationship continues to believe that the agreement to be faithful is in force and lives a life that testifies to this fact, while the other partner is secretly violating it by living a life of deception, sin, and sex outside marriage.

Adultery is not simply a wrong action, but it is also a violation of God's divine order for marriage. A person who has had an affair must seek his spouse's forgiveness for the adulterous act and also for violating the marriage covenant; the sacred commitment. The sacred covenant creates an atmosphere of security and trust. That security and trust is what wives need in order to give themselves freely to their husbands. Only a restored sense of security and trust; asking and receiving forgiveness for breaking the covenant, can begin to restore confidence, peace and joy to the wounded spouse.

The wounded spouse will struggle with multiple issues and it is important to realize this. Her own sexual identity has become confused. She is asking deep in her soul, what is wrong with me that he would want someone else? Shame emerges in her spirit: shame that he would want any other woman. Although she forgives his acts, she needs to process and eventually forgive him for the ways she has been affected by his violation of their marriage vows.

It may appear that one's behavior is the problem, and that a promise "to change" is the solution but, the real problem with someone is the fact that in his mind, he granted himself permission to break his marriage vows. Without getting to the real problem, both spouses are destined to continue feeling as though something is wrong, but neither will understand what. They will continue to struggle wondering why their relationship is so tentative and distant.

Trust will be difficult to restore, a couple cannot know intimacy without trust. "To set the stage for restored trust, he must be able to humbly admit that he is unable to manage his sin or keep his promises, and that he is deeply addicted to the pleasure of sin. At that point, he will be in a position to receive God's freeing grace and empowerment to choose differently. By being humble and openly dependent on God, he will also be putting himself in a position where she can begin to trust him again. As renewed trust grows between them, the couple will be able to enjoy rich intimacy, true fulfillment and sustaining joy. By conquering these hurdles together, hurting spouses can overcome the damage of infidelity. By learning to trust God in a new, much deeper way, they can enjoy a stronger, more fulfilling marriage."

Affairs, both physical and emotional, are devastating. The damage done after the discovery or revelation of an affair can destroy a marriage and family. It is generally far better to prevent an affair from happening. Some marriages are destroyed by infidelity. While the damage may be irreparable, fortunately, this is not always the case. Some couples are willing to commit the time and effort to save their relationship. Recovery after cheating isn't easy, but it can be done if both parties are willing to make reconciliation a priority.

Rebuilding a relationship after an affair, while certainly possible, can take a long time, and in some cases, may be unattainable.

**Step 1**: Decide whether you are willing to continue with the marriage if your spouse agrees to stop the infidelity. You must be able to forgive the cheating if your partner is willing to break off the affair and take steps to ensure it never happens again. This means you cannot bring it up every time you have a fight or hold it over your spouse's head whenever you get upset.

**Step 2**: Confront your spouse about the cheating. Focus on facts so your partner won't automatically go on the defensive. Own your feelings with statements like, "I feel hurt and betrayed," instead of making judgments like, "You are a total jerk," which will quickly shut the conversation down.

**Step 3**: Agree to a time-out period. You will need to focus a lot of time and energy on repair efforts if your partner agrees to try to salvage the marriage. Emotions will initially run high, so the Mayo Clinic recommends giving each other some space before starting the hard work. Agree on a mutually acceptable time period, such as a week or two, that will allow you both to approach the situation more rationally.

**Step 4**: Make mutual goals. Both you and your partner will benefit from focusing on reasons to salvage the marriage. Your goals might involve your children, future financial or retirement plans or anything else that binds you together in a positive way. Find divine help through prayer. Take steps to change the factors that led the unfaithful to cheat and work together to fix the problem.

**Step 5**: Agree to safeguards that help you regain trust in your partner. You may want to be able to check emails or cell phone records on request. Your spouse should agree to provide this access without complaint. Create understanding. Apologize effectively. Explain point of view. Make promises and follow through on them. Promises need to be mutually agreed upon; they must be reasonable, that they can be lived up to and they must be explicitly clear. The how, when, what and where need to be understood.

**Step 6**: Set up marriage counseling sessions to help you both create and implement a plan to repair the marriage. A counselor gives an unbiased viewpoint and helps you and your spouse identify factors that led to the infidelity, find other potential issues in the marriage and create strategies to strengthen your relationship.

# Chapter IX

## TIPS AND WARNINGS FOR REBUILDING

It takes time and hard work to fully deal with marital infidelity, but the American Association for Marriage and Family Therapy states there are several signs when things are on the right track. The marriage should be getting stronger and focused on couple hood, and problems should be addressed as they come up. You should be rebuilding trust and commitment slowly but surely, and both you and your partner should be demonstrating empathy for each other.

You are likely to get through the crisis and save the marriage if you see these things happening. It is important not to give up out of frustration because it seems to be taking longer than you thought. Trust takes a long time to rebuild because our negative emotions tend to stay with us longer than our positive emotions. Trust is easy to lose and hard to regain, Rebuilding trust requires a lot of understanding and commitment from both sides.

Honor your spouse by honoring your marriage vow of fidelity. Remember the commitment you and your spouse have made to one another. Frame a copy of your wedding vows and hang it someplace where you can see it daily as a gentle reminder of the vows you took. Fidelity is a decision and you and your spouse need to understand that you both intend to practice it.

Be aware of infidelity "danger zones." The workplace and the Internet can be dangerous to your marriage. Many people that engage in affairs meet at work or online.

Katherine Robredo, LCSW, a marriage and family therapist and Nathan Woods give the following suggestions in their article "Preventing Infidelity". Many jobs these days involve traveling, often with male and female colleagues going on business trips together. If there is a person from work that you feel you may develop an attraction for, protect your marriage by not spending time alone with that person. At work, or while traveling, socialize in groups. Be disciplined about your behavior in working relationships.

Again, do not disclose too much personal information to people at work. If you are having problems in your marriage, discuss this with a counselor not a friend or colleague of the opposite sex. A good rule of thumb in terms of preventing an affair is to ask yourself "would I be doing or saying this if my spouse was here?" If the answer is "no," then you may be treading into the danger zone of infidelity.

Online relationships can be very dangerous to a marriage. Many marriages today are damaged by "emotional affairs" which occur via email, chat rooms, or other Web-based forums. Having a close friendship with a member of the opposite sex can sometimes lead to an emotional affair. Some indications of an emotional affair include sharing inappropriate or intimate thoughts or personal information, talking in detail about your marriage in a negative way, and keeping the relationship secret from your spouse.

An "emotional affair" is often just as devastating to a marriage as a physical affair. In each case, one spouse has turned away from their partner, is being dishonest and is violating trust and honor in the marriage. Prevent online affairs by keeping the computer in a shared room such as a family room or kitchen where the screen cannot be hidden from your spouse. Avoid chat rooms and discussing emotional topics and personal or marital problems with people over the Internet.

Know yourself and create open lines of communication with your spouse.

**Honestly assess if you may be vulnerable to an affair.**

Ask yourself if you are angry with your spouse; you feel resentful; find it hard to communicate; or you feel disconnected. Any of these feelings can make you more susceptible to an affair.

### Discuss your concerns with your partner

Meet with a couple's counselor together to learn how to approach difficult subjects.

### Consider taking a marriage education class

It will teach you good communication and <u>conflict management</u> skills. These can give you the skills you and your spouse need to have these conversations.

### Discuss together how to "affair-proof" your marriage.

Find out what your partner is comfortable with in regard to relationships with members of the opposite sex and set guidelines for how each of you will behave in these situations. For example, you may agree that neither of you goes to dinner alone with a colleague while traveling for work.

### Discuss the boundaries and expectations of your marriage in terms of fidelity.

Discuss with your spouse whenever you are feeling attracted to another person. The myth that once we are married we will never be attracted to anyone else can be very damaging and can create a lot of personal feelings of guilt and shame if not expressed. People in happy marriages may occasionally be attracted to someone else. By mutually acknowledging this they can redirect themselves and be reminded of their boundaries and commitment to their marriage. By not discussing these issues, they become "secret" and it becomes easier to get involved in an affair.

### Make your marriage a priority.

Life is very busy and it is easy to get caught up in work and children and other things that consume your time and energy. Many people let their marriage fall lower on the priority list and take their spouse for granted. Set aside daily time to reconnect with your spouse. A cup of coffee together in the morning, a time alone to talk in the evening, a weekly lunch date or a walk together after dinner are some simple ways to stay connected. The amount of quiet time together does not have to be huge, but spending 15-20 minutes a day alone together will help to keep your marriage on track.

**Create a marriage vision.**

Take some time alone and write a very specific vision of what a great marriage looks like to you. After each partner defines their own vision, they should share this vision with each other and discuss why each element is important. Using each of their "visions" the couple can then create a "shared vision." Write this up, decorate it and hang it in a place where it will be seen every day. This will remind you daily of your shared goals, aspirations and future within the marriage.

**Make time for doing fun things in the marriage.**

The simple idea of "a family that plays together, stays together" is true. Having fun and laughing together helps keep your relationship strong. It is easy to get bogged down with the business of life and many couples do not make time for fun. Make a list of things you enjoy doing together and make sure to do at least two things from the list each month. Continually add to your list and make sure it has a variety of activities to meet any budget.

Extra-marital affairs don't "just happen." Engaging in an affair can have devastating consequences that affect your life forever. There are clear steps and choices that lead into an affair. By following the above tips you can "affair proof" your marriage and prevent infidelity before it begins. Romantic betrayal is traumatizing, says psychologist Joshua Coleman. But couples can learn to trust again.

Discovering a partner's affair can be devastating because it strikes at so many aspects of one's identity. It can cause the betrayed person to doubt their own attractiveness or judgment in people. This is because our relationships are built upon the fragile agreement that those about whom we care most deeply will behave, in large part, as they have always behaved. A betrayal can shatter that trust and open the door to the possibility that things in one's small, intimate world may not be as they appear.

The roots of these feelings stretch back to childhood, when we need predictability in the care we receive. A great deal of research suggests that when a baby's need for predictability is not met, that baby can grow into an anxious and distrusting adult. As children, we will even irrationally blame problems on ourselves instead of our parents as a way to make the world feel more orderly and predictable. Trust always entails the suspension of disbelief. This is, in part, why betrayals can be so psychologically traumatizing. It's as if one's entire view of the world has been proven false. In fact, studies show that psychological traumas like discovering an affair have the capacity to affect brain functioning long after the event occurs. One of these changes is the development of a hyper-vigilance to further assaults.

Unfortunately, hyper-vigilance exists primarily to put the individual on global red alert that danger is afoot. It creates a suspicion of future betrayals and tempts us to look for lies elsewhere—in other family members, co-workers, or spiritual leaders. Yet this distrust is often misplaced. It limits the strength and the number of our social connections, often leaving us isolated from the rest of the world. This is why it is urgent for us to learn how to trust again, even if one's relationship is destroyed. Trust isn't just essential to relationships; it's necessary for a happy, meaningful life. Couples who commit to working on their relationships often find they are much stronger as a result.

## Rebuilding trust

If you are the person who has been betrayed by an affair, rebuilding trust can be extremely difficult even though it can also bring several rewards. While not every betrayal is caused by a problem in the marriage, the betrayed person can use the crisis of betrayal to better understand his or her partner, and this understanding can help reduce the probability that the traumatic behavior will occur again—a vital step toward rebuilding trust.

This isn't about maintaining a romance and also about friendship. John Gottman, one of nation's top marriage experts, has found that couples who retain a strong friendship throughout their romantic relationship are the ones who have the most lasting partnerships. "Friendship demands that partners be willing to understand each other's inner world—their needs, desires, motivations, and sense of well-being."

The betrayer must be willing to give the betrayed a sense of control, while the betrayed person must try to find that control. More advice to survive infidelity:

## Avoid humiliating your partner.

You have to decide whether you want revenge or a relationship. You can't have both—at least not for very long. "If you fail to allow your partner to make sincere amends, there's a greater chance your relationship will end. Dr. Gottman has found that when individuals don't allow their partners to repair the damage caused by marital conflict, they increase the chance of divorce."

## Separate out complaints from criticism.

"Your relationship will heal more quickly if you communicate your complaints in a way that makes your partner motivated to re-establish trust. Shame, humiliation, and criticism are counter-productive because they cause the other to shut down, avoid, and retreat." Researcher Martin Seligman advises that people try to think of their partners' flaws in non-absolute terms. For example, try to see the affair as a terrible mistake, one which you may or may not have had some complicity creating.

**Isolate the times that you talk about the betrayal.**

A betrayal can become a 24/7 topic of conversation. This can be damaging to both parties. Agree upon a time to check in on the topic. The person who has been betrayed should make the decision about when to reduce the frequency of the conversations. Someone needs to start the healing process. Pray for God to give you graciousness to take the first step to make matters right.

**Evaluate whether you have the capacity to forgive your partner.**

"It is possible that the wound is too deep and that the betrayer too flawed to ever again be worthy of trust." In order to determine whether you should work to restore trust in your partner, ask yourself: Is this a new behavior, or part of an ongoing pattern of untrustworthiness? If it's not part of an ongoing pattern, work with your partner to heal the betrayal.

"Ask if your partner seems genuinely motivated to change, or just motivated not to feel guilty. Your hurt and angry feelings may make it difficult for you to read him or her correctly. In addition, the fact that your trust was violated may make you less able to take your partner's words at face value. After betrayal, it is legitimate to be able to look at phone records, emails, and cell phone logs in order to feel reassured that there is congruence between what your partner says and does." Feeling there's consistency between what your partner says and does is critical to rebuilding trust and maintaining your sanity. However, this is a short-term strategy and shouldn't be considered a substitute for the harder part of negotiating true, long-term trust.

**Get help**

"After a romantic betrayal, it is common for people to avoid reaching out to their usual support system because they don't want to share their shame or humiliation. As a result, betrayal begets isolation." It's not just about preserving the relationship: when you've been betrayed, you might need help to control the damage caused to your individual identity, your self-esteem, and your feelings of security in the world.

## Making amends

If you have betrayed someone you love, the following steps are crucial.

### Take complete responsibility for your actions.

Taking responsibility when you make mistakes is a key part of marital friendship. "The most important predictor of rebuilding trust after an affair, other than love, is the capacity for both members of the couple to take some responsibility for what happened." This can be very difficult for the person who was betrayed, but it is a step that must be taken if the relationship is to be saved. Establishing mutual responsibility and regaining a sense of control are a big part of rebuilding trust. It is based upon the principle that we are not victims of our partner's whims, nor are we victims of our own mistakes; we can actually do something to improve the relationship.

The more you blame your partner, the longer it will take him or her to believe that you are trustworthy and to want to forgive you. Pride stands between you and forgiveness. Repent-reverse your thinking completely. Reposition yourself into God's way of thinking and His way of doing things. Be truthful about faults in actions and personality. Healthy thinking is a habit, just like neurotic thinking is a habit, and healthy habits are learned in the same way as unhealthy ones—through practice. Developing your psychological strength is just like developing your physical abilities—the more you exercise the stronger you become.

### Assume it will take time for your partner to heal.

Your feelings of guilt, shame, or humiliation may make you reluctant to raise the topic of the affair or cause you to close down the conversation prematurely. Don't assume that it will take at least a year for your partner to be able to trust you again. You should be prepared to maintain ongoing, sometimes painful conversations about your betrayal. You may also need support from close friends or a therapist.

**Be empathic.**

"Your guilt and shame may make you uncomfortable listening to how badly you've made your partner feel. However, it is critical that you show empathy and make amends for how much hurt you've caused your partner. This is because empathy is an expression of care and concern. Showing that you are willing to bear your feelings of guilt, remorse, or fear of losing your partner—without blaming back or cutting off the conversation—will go a long way to proving that you are someone worth trusting again."

**Respect the need for new limits or rules.**

Your partner has good reason to be more suspicious. Accept that there should now be more transparency around emails, phone logs, and so on. Your relationship will heal more quickly as you become less defensive and trust will be re-established.

**Show enthusiasm for change and repair.**

If you really want to be trusted, you will have to demonstrate that you are in it for the long haul. The person who committed the betrayal may have to change jobs or even move out of the area as a way to show his or her dedication to saving the relationship. Rebuilding trust after a betrayal isn't easy but most couples who succeed find that their relationships are much stronger for the effort. A happy life requires us to heal the wounds of the past. It also requires a willingness to see that the future may not resemble the past at all.

John Gottman, explains why trust is essential to couples and communities—and how we can build it. In this excerpt from his talk, he discusses his trailblazing work on the science of trust, exploring its importance for couples and communities alike. He has studied what makes marriages work for over 40 years. He found that the number one most important issue that came up to couples was trust and betrayal.

"Can I trust you to be there and listen to me when I'm upset? Can I trust you to choose me over your mother, over your friends? Can I trust you to work for our family? To not take drugs? Can I trust you to not cheat on me and be sexually faithful? Can I trust you to respect me, to help with things in the house to really be involved with our children?" Trust is one of the most commonly used words in the English language—it is essential to healthy relationships and healthy communities. Trust isn't just important for couples. Trust is central to what makes human communities work.

## Building trust

In any interaction, there is a possibility of connecting with your partner or turning away from your partner. Dan Yoshimoto (John Gottman's graduate student) has discovered that the basis for building trust is really the idea of attunement. He has broken this down with the acronym ATTUNE, which stands for:

- Awareness of your partner's emotion;
- Turning toward the emotion;
- Tolerance of two different viewpoints;
- trying to Understand your partner;
- Non-defensive responses to your partner;
- and responding with Empathy.

# CHAPTER X

## THE EFFECTS OF TECHNOLOGY ON RELATIONSHIPS

Technology has caused behaviors to change and relationships are being threatened. It distracts couples from each other and when used excessively robs each of the opportunity to be totally intimate. Facebook, the Internet and other social media provide a sense of instant gratification that stimulates our brain's reward centers, offering quick hits of novelty that can be downright addictive. They allow us to connect with friends, co-workers, and even former flames, fostering an immediate and intense sense of intimacy that can lead us to romanticize these connections. At best, you're giving your energy to these digital distractions, not your partner. At worst, you could be setting the stage for emotional infidelity.

If we observe people at the restaurants we must admit that there is a large group on their cell phones; talking, texting, playing games while there are others at the same table bored or on their laptops, iPads or tablets. If this is the scene in public places, can you imagine what the scene is like at the homes? Safeguards must be implemented. Times need to be set apart to turn off the television, Computers, cell phones, iPads etc. and focus 100 percent on spouses and family members.

The cell phone has become more and more a part of everyone's life. Now with the smartphones we can stay connected 24/7, checking and responding to emails, socializing on Facebook or Twitter and reach anyone around the world at any time of the day and almost from anywhere. How much time is spent on cell phones as compared to the time spent with the spouse? "Andrew K. Przbylski and Netta Weinstein Researchers from the University of Essex found that our phones can hurt close relationships. People who engaged in personal discussions when a cell phone was nearby—even if neither was actually using it—reported lower relationship quality and less trust for their partner. They also felt their partner was less empathetic to their concerns." A recent survey by Mobile Mindset found that three out of five U.S. Smartphone users don't go more than an hour without checking their gadgets. (Smartphones, tablets and laptops).

Cell phones and Computers are used to sustain extramarital relationships and online chat rooms to find and build new relationships which can lead to emotional affairs. These tools are ruling lives and causing havoc on family life. The truth is, however, that even a "virtual" affair can wreak havoc on a marriage or a serious dating relationship. The growing influence and availability of the Internet has only made things worse, with as many as one in 10 Internet users reporting that they are addicted to cybersex or other online temptations. After all, online sexual encounters offer the thrill of a make-believe romance along with the added benefit of anonymity. And because many online affairs don't involve actual physical contact, participants can convince themselves that cybersex isn't really adulterous, that they aren't really cheating on their spouse.

"Ever since the Internet has become a regular part of the human experience, cyberspace has been implicated as an accomplice in online affairs, real life adultery, and the break-up marriages. It has made the survival of marriage even more difficult. A new realm of opportunities and threats now surrounds couples and their relationship and creates unneeded pressure in the marriage. The Internet can be a source of pornography, erotic fantasy, illicit relationships, cyber affairs and ultimately the destruction of marriages. According to a report by the American Association for Marriage and Family Therapy, between 20 and 33 percent of Internet users in the United States go online for sexual purposes—either to view pornographic images or to engage in an online sexual relationship of some kind. Most of these are married men; as many as 17 percent of users become addicted to online sexual activity.

It is dangerous to replace conversation with connectivity. We lose emotions, facial expressions, tone of voice and much more. Real relationships require real conversation and real emotions. God intended for us to experience the sound of our voices, the body language and the touch as a vital part of relating love and having communion with others. Implementing boundaries will promote face-to-face communication in marriages.

## Set it Aside

Turn the gadget off and keep it out of sight put it in your bag or your pocket. Shut them off at night and put them in another room to charge at night.

## No devices at the dinner table

Dinner time is a perfect time for face-to-face conversation. "TTT-Timeout from Technology at the Table.

## No phones at the restaurant

Do not use phones unless it is to call the babysitter. Also, stay away from restaurants that have televisions. This is a distraction device. Use this time to reconnect with family and have real conversation.

## No texting or talking about important personal issues over the phone.

Important issues need to be discussed face-to-face to avoid misunderstandings. For the LUV communication to be effective we must observe body language, hear the tone of voice and be able to understand and validate in person. (Exceptions only when the matter can't wait)

These boundaries may be difficult at first if you or a family member has an addiction to technology, but the effort will pay off in the long run with improved family relationships. All these boundaries establish a strong family value: When you're with someone, that relationship is your priority. Anything that becomes a necessity has the ability to become an idol." You can become so attached to your smartphone that it basically becomes the most important thing in your life: "If you can't live without a gadget . . . throw it away. If a gadget is absorbing most of your leisure times . . . throw it away!

Spouses are crying and screaming out because of the choices their partners are making which are destroying their marriages. It's almost at epidemic proportions. Most of these are good Christians, afterward confessing, "I/we never meant for this to happen." Yet it did and it does. And as a result innocent hearts are breaking. The ultimate threat is not the latest technology . . . it is the choices you make online and offline . . . in cyberspace and real life".

"Instead of just fighting about money or how frequently to have sex, couples are also fighting about time spent on Facebook or whether it's OK to send a text during a romantic dinner or bring a laptop on a getaway weekend," says marriage expert Howard Markman. This is a wakeup call, we MUST protect our marriages from the sneakiness and secrecy that is going on, centering on Internet and cell phones that is destroying relationships everywhere.

"In the final book of the Old Testament, Malachi 2 talks about setting up a protective perimeter around the covenant relationship, so guard the spirit of marriage within you. Don't cheat on your spouse. "The man who hates and divorces his wife,", "does violence to the one he should protect, says the LORD Almighty.

"One of the boundaries is that neither of you be alone with someone of the opposite sex to avoid the appearance of impropriety or being caught in a potential he said/she said situation. Here are some "dos and don'ts" for Facebooking couples.

**DO'S**

- DO Create boundaries to protect yourself, your

spouse and your marriage.

- DO Set your relationship status to Married and keep it that way.
- DO Choose Your Friends Wisely
- DO Discuss with your mate: What Facebook friends and groups are inbounds or out-of-bounds?
- DO Update each other on your Facebook Friends and Friend Requests.
- DO Share your username and password with one another.
- DO Make your spouse the topic of your Status Updates at least once a week
- DO Be prepared to talk offline about online issues."
- DO Play it Smart With Who You Talk About What With
- DO If in Doubt, De-friend Them." Great boundaries!"

**DON'TS**

- DON'T write cutting remarks or negative statements about your spouse.
- DON'T Friend exes, old flames, past flings, former crushes or anyone you've been intimate within the past.
- DON'T lose track of how much time you spend on Facebook.
- DON'T Report that you or your spouse is out of town.
- DON'T have private Chat sessions with people of the opposite sex.
- DON'T Let Facebook be a distraction during your time with your mate."

These principles can be applied to other Internet and Cell Phone activities in various ways. "Create boundaries to protect yourself, your spouse and your marriage." It's the secrecy matter and the poor choices that spouses are making in HOW they use their time and WITH WHOM, which threatens peace and sanctity in marriages today.

And then there's the whole "private" thing where calls can be made and/or taken in secrecy. Some spouses keep cell phones to themselves, warning that they're "off limits" to their mate (or they purchase them without letting their wife/husband know so secrecy and falling into or deliberately giving into sexual temptation is easier). This type of behavior is a HUGE red flag that something is wrong in the marriage. If a spouse doesn't have anything to hide, he or she won't need to hide anything. Cell phone and computer privacy shouldn't be an issue for a couple that are supposed to "be one."

So, with that in mind, so you don't "separate" that which God joined together when you married and you build a marriage where each of you shows you are a trustworthy partner, the following is good advice from Dr. Willard Harley: "there are many steps couples can take to shield their marriage from secrecy and infidelity, for instance, couples should have each other's cell-phone and e-mail information 'at their disposal.' If there already has been an infidelity problem, a couple should review e-mails together before erasing them, he said. 'Trust, to me, is earned, not assumed.' Keep in mind the words from Hebrews 13,

> "Marriage should be honored by all, and the marriage
> bed kept pure, for God will judge the adulterer and all
> the sexually immoral."

Please try to work with your spouse to protect your relationship now while you can, if you can. Bring things out into the open and keep them there. Trouble grows in darkness and secrecy. It can be the enemy of our faith's playground. If your spouse will not work with you to protect your marriage and stop secrecy, pray, pray, pray and keep asking God for wisdom. You do and will need the help and guidance of our Wonderful Counselor, the Holy Spirit.

> "May the God who gives endurance and encouragement

give you the same attitude of mind toward each other that Christ Jesus had, so that with one mind and one voice you may glorify the God and Father of our Lord Jesus Christ. (Romans 15:5-6)

## Pornography

Technology has allowed easy and free access to pornography. Many people who would not purchase pornography if they had to do so in a public place feel free to access it in the privacy of their own home. There have been numerous studies on how the increase in pornography has been damaging. Marriages can be negatively impacted and in some cases, divorce results from one person's interest in online pornography or from their online sexualized behaviors.

Pornography stimulates a distorted view of sexuality within the porn addict that can lead to the desire for riskier, more perverse and even criminal sexual behaviors. It damages the trust and intimacy within the husband-wife relationship, which often leads to the end of the marriage. The spouse of the sex addict can develop deep emotional wounds and feelings of betrayal, loss, devastation and anger.

When you are faced with these kinds of issues in your marriage, how can you handle them?

- Find a spiritual person that can be a prayer partner for you.
- Pray for your spouse's deliverance and be as supportive as possible. Please understand that being supportive does not mean to be in denial or ignore any issues.
- The person with the issue must make amends. Making amends includes finding an accountability partner, being completely open with all information.
- If you need more support, join a group and/or find a church to attend.

# CHAPTER XI

## MAKE YOUR MARRIAGE MORE IMPORTANT THAN MONEY

"People are made to be loved and things are made to be used. The confusion in this world is that people are used and things are loved."—Author Unknown.

Modern society has placed an enormous emphasis on the accumulation of material things. Its mass media stimulated appetites and it's keeping up with the Joneses (or the Kardashians, the television reality show) have taken over the households in America. How much stuff do we really need to be happy? Does stuff make a family happy?

**Financial Problems**

Economic strain is something that all married couples are subjected to at some point or other in life. While some couples are understanding enough to make it through, others give in to such marital problems. What starts as a minor argument initially goes a long way—only to end with separation. Money is the most common source of conflict between husbands and wives. Many domestic arguments happen because couples are struggling financially. The struggles are usually because of the worries over bills that need to be paid. Research has shown that materialistic people compared to those who don't care much about possessions are unhappier.

Two of the major sources of conflict are the value conditioning that each of the mates has had in his childhood and the complex of anxieties, attitudes, and behaviors that make up each partner's personality. The differential childhood conditioning about money is one of the most common problems. General attitudes toward spending and earning money and some specific habits of how and what to purchase are acquired in childhood.

According to Jason Carroll, a Professor of Family Life at Brigham Young University, you will have a happier marriage if a materialistic person marries someone who isn't. In the studies he and his colleagues found the more materialistic you are, the more you suffer anxiety, depression, and insecurity than non-materialistic types. Materialistic people tend to put work first at the cost of their intimate relationships. The research done through the RELATE Institute, which is a respected national research non-profit organization, studied 1,734 married couples. The marriages with at least one materialistic spouse were worse off on all measures than marriages where neither spouse was materialistic.

## Attitudes towards Money

Money is a leading cause of marital strife. When one spouse is a saver and the other likes to overspend, a lot of conflict is created, especially during the difficult financial times some spenders comfort themselves by overspending.

People who have to scrimp to make ends meet may be very tight with money or go spend it foolishly. If the partner was indulged in every whim, he may have no appreciation of the true value of money and may be self-centered. One who had to work or live within a strict budget may have a greater regard for money and use it wisely.

Insecurity is a big problem in spending the family income, but immaturity is even worse. Not all immature couples are teenagers. There are some husbands and wives who try to use money to control the other person. Some men don't even let their wives know how much they make. The male who behaves this way is unsure of his role and fears that sharing spending decisions with his wife will somehow diminish his male status. Some males use money as a form of punishment, denying a wife who hasn't behaved the way he thinks she should some of the things she wants. There are cases where in which women who come from higher income families buy or attempt to buy the affection or the adherence of their less well-to-do husbands. There are also wives who punish their husbands for some insult, either real or imagined, by just going out and spending.

Financial freedom is all about creating alternative sources of income so that you do not have to work for the money—let the money work for you and make more money. By seeing the big picture and agreeing upon the goals together, you can lay a strong foundation for your finances in marriage. Develop a budget together. With a budget you will know each other's expectations in every aspect of spending. Agree together on who manages each part of the budget. Some areas you may decide to equally manage. Sometimes the husband feels that his income is "his" because he earns it. Often a wife who works outside the home believes that the additional income should belong to her and that she should have absolute control over its expenditure, despite the fact that her husband is paying all the family bills out of his income.

Make it a priority for each of you to have some "fun money" to spend any way that you want without reporting it to your spouse. You can budget some money for this or you can fund it with gifts or unexpected earnings. Divide the financial responsibilities according to strengths and time availability. Decide who should pay the bills, balance the checkbook, and keep track of investments. Have a joint checking account. Make some time each month to discuss your finances together. Use this opportunity to monitor the budget and spending, discuss your progress toward financial goals, and address other issues that surface.

Because of our affluent society's emphasis on instant gratification and the desire to begin marriages at the same level as one's parents now have, newlyweds often buy expensive appliances and automobiles; Sometimes without figuring out the total monthly payments and the relationship of those payments to their income. An

98

unexpected pregnancy, an illness, the loss of a job, or any one of a hundred other emergencies can put them on the financial rocks. If this happens, the damage to their credit rating is bad enough, but the damage to their marriage relationship may be even worse. Soon they may be blaming each other for their financial mess.

Most families that are financially successful have some common characteristics. These families have goals, both long range and short range. Next they are able to plan ahead because they are motivated to set aside present desire in deference to long range satisfactions. They usually work out for themselves some system of spending that is acceptable to its members. Here are five common systems to be used for the allocation of the money.

- The Dole system: one family member hands out the money a little bit at a time to the other. If it is not fully accepted by the partners, it can make for constant conflict.
- The family treasurer system: family members get a personal allowance. The rest is turned over to the treasurer who pays all the bills and does most of the buying.
- Division of Expenses System: Certain spending is assigned to the husband (ex. Rent, car, or insurance) and the other spending is the responsibility of the wife (food, utility or clothing). Additional spending is done by cooperative decision.
- Joint Account System: earnings of both husband and wife are put in a joint checking account from which either may draw to pay common or personal expenses. One partner or the other writes the checks for the household bills. This system works well when both members are responsible and cooperative individuals and when the income consistently runs above the expenses.
- The last is the budget system: the best for most families. Expenses are budgeted in advance by

common agreement. Any excess goes into a common fund that is saved or spent only by common agreement. Many people think the budget is a device for saving, in reality it is a plan for spending. It enables people to decide in advance what they want to spend their money for and then to be sure there is enough left to purchase those satisfactions previously agreed upon. The budget helps families to look at the whole spending picture and weigh short range satisfactions against long range goals.

Priorities for Financial Fulfillment
- Pay God first.
- Start an Emergency Fund.
- Pay off Debts from smallest to largest.
- Expand your savings.
- Start Investing in your Retirement.
- Set aside funds to help pay for your children's college education.
- Pay off your house.
- Give extra generously.

The non-materialistic couples were 10%—15% better off in the categories studied (marital satisfaction, marriage stability, and lower levels of conflict). Dr. Carroll and his team believe materialism erodes marriage because:

"Materialism causes spouses to make bad financial decisions such as spending beyond their means, which puts them in debt and stresses the marriage.

People who are materialistic are working more to "get things." They forget to take out time for the relationship; don't value the relationship; or run out of time in a day to nurture the relationship."

## Tips to Put Marriage over Money

- No matter how hard you work, if you communicate with your spouse each day, letting them know something as simple as, "I am thinking about you," you will be nurturing your relationship.

- Balance is everything. At times that is difficult and unattainable. When you know in advance that work will be consuming a lot of your time, tell your partner in advance so they can mentally prepare. Take them to dinner or spend extra time with them prior to the week or month that you need to focus on work. Remind them by saying something such as, "I am glad we have this time together, because next week (or next month) is going to be very demanding at work." This tells your partner they are more important to you than money.

- Have a family day. One day a week sacred to families. Shut all communication off on that day. Program that day into your iPhone or whatever device you have so you won't schedule business.

- Husbands, wives, and children all like nice things, but they love you. Their love is a gift, not something you will get paid for. No amount of money or nice things you can ever acquire will replace this love.

- As a family, it's nice to have a charity to which you give every year. Let the kids be part of planning which charity means the most to them. Teaching your children early to value life rather than material is very important.

- We all like nice things, but when they are valued more than our loved ones, it becomes a downhill ride.

## Changes in Income

If the household income is dwindling—perhaps one spouse got laid off or credit card interest is eating a larger chunk of the budget—Dr.

Wilcox says it can rob a couple of a sense of their future together, because they don't have any money to put into savings for long-term goals like a trip or a house down payment. Instead, they're worrying about cash flow and paying off debt, which looms over their marriage like a storm cloud."

The job loss or salary reduction of the husband can be devastating, but even if it's the wife's. "Even though there's been a great deal of change in contemporary families, there's still the implicit expectation that the husband will be the primary breadwinner. If he isn't able to do that, it's a huge blow to his self-esteem," says Dr. Wilcox. If the husband feels that his role as provider is being threatened, he might become resentful or turn to drugs, alcohol or affairs as a way of escaping the economic pressures at home, Dr. Wilcox adds.

The wife, too, might become resentful—especially if she's still going to work every day on top of doing most of the child care and housework. "If the husband has trouble finding another job, he may become discouraged and lose his motivation for seeking employment. To the wife, this can seem like a broken promise, because he is no longer trying to be the provider," says James Craig, Ph.D., a marriage and family therapist.

No one can predict exactly how a couple might react to financial stressors. Some people might yell, argue or blame each other. Some might turn within themselves and become more anxious, depressed and withdrawn while others may just walk out on the marriage physically or emotionally. "Any behavior that puts distance between you and your partner—you stop talking, you pull back, you're not interacting, you're not showing affection, you're not having sexual contact—is going to be detrimental," warns Larry Barlow, Ph.D., coordinator of the Center for Couple and Family Therapy at Florida State University. "So now, not only are your finances in bad shape, your marriage is too."

Crown Financial Ministries in an article in Focus on the Family website; suggests a husband's and wife's incomes in marriage should be merged and shared. Someone should be in charge of keeping a budget for the household, and whatever funds there are should be held mutually. This will require a lot of faith in the Lord, as well as in your spouse. Advice: Don't forget to ask God what He wants you to do with your money. He made you stewards over your finances for a purpose, so you should always remember to ask what His plans are. Many blessings can come from appropriate money management in marriage.

## Make Decisions Together

If you agree to come to mutual decisions on how the finances are handled, this will strengthen trust between you and your partner. Commit to making important decisions together. Major financial decisions are best decided as a couple. One of the greatest areas of strain in a marriage is the sphere of finances. Discuss your finances on a regular basis, even if one of you is better at handling the practical aspects, like paying the bills and balancing the check book. Keeping secrets about spending will drive a wedge between a couple faster than anything. Also, you won't be able to keep secrets from each other if you commit to making all important family decisions together. This is one of the best ways to develop trust as a couple.

# CHAPTER XII

## STRESS IN MARRIAGE

Husbands and wives face many pressures today. What can they do to manage them to be sure their marriages survive? Couples who have been married for a while have their stories about the tough times and the hardships they have been through. Husbands and wives have faced hardships—problems that affect their relationship. Psychologists have labeled these difficulties as marriage stressors: any kind of external influence, circumstance or event that challenges or threatens a marriage. Some marital stressors cause husbands and wives to just gradually drift apart—with little or no conflict between them. Be aware of life's stressors and don't let them drive you and your partner apart.

Finances, unemployment, infidelity, intimacy difficulties, parenting views, the death of a child, chronic health issues, dependent family member and in-law clashes are some of the stressors which have been identified to cause problems in the marriage. Couples argue about how to spend their money and argue about who is working harder to keep the household budget in the black. The impact of the unemployment rate where it is and the down economy, salary reductions, high cost of living, unbelievably high credit card debt, falling home values and disappearing retirement accounts, have tremendously increased the stress in the marriages.

Frenetic lifestyle is taking a huge toll on marriage too. Many couples today have overloaded their schedules with work, child care, child activities and household responsibilities, as well as recreational pursuits and social functions. After they've given their energy to all of these demands and commitments, they don't have much left over for each other or even to just rest and unwind.

Marriages and families need to spend more time with each other, but "with so many of them, they just can't fit 'couple time' or 'family time' into their busy schedules. "Just about every couple lives under unending pressures and demands that cause them to be overcommitted and overextended." Has life always been this hectic? No! Life hasn't always been so hectic. According to research done by Becky Sweat; "Back in the 1970s, about two thirds of married couples had a spouse at home (usually the wife). All the domestic responsibilities could get taken care of during the weekdays. But today, only 40 percent of families have a stay-at-home spouse."

Couples now work a combined average of 63 hours a week, up from just 52.5 in 1970, according to a 2009 report on workplace flexibility from the Georgetown University Law Center. With both parents working so many hours away from home, many feel they have no choice but to use weeknights and weekends to run errands and do housekeeping tasks that didn't get done during the weekdays. When marital partners work different schedules, couple time becomes even harder to come by. Some to save on child care costs have rearranged their work schedules where one will work the day shift while the other works nights and their schedules may overlap for only a short time each day.

Today, one in four dual-earner American couples have a spouse working the late-night or rotating, nonstandard shifts. Typically these jobs require at least some weekend work. Such schedules undermine the stability of marriages, increase the amount of housework to be done, reduce family cohesiveness and require elaborate child care arrangements.

Couples in which one spouse works a late shift report having substantially less quality time together and more marital unhappiness than couples where spouses work only fixed daytime jobs. These couples are also more likely to separate or divorce.

On top of complicated work schedules, parents often have their children involved in a wide range of extracurricular activities.

"Weekends used to be a time for families to just kick back and relax together." Now the parents are busy all weekend shuffling their kids to all the different sporting events they're involved with. Add to this frenzied schedule parents individual hobbies and recreation, long hunting weekends, baseball games, gal's nights out, etc.

If most parents were not already overbooked with children's activities, perhaps the adult activities would not be such a concern. But in truth, between chauffeuring kids and being personally involved in two or three adult activities, you know what will come last in your life—your marriage.

We feel accountable to our children and the commitments we have made to and for them. We feel accountable to our friends, the club we promised to attend monthly, to the committees we joined, and to the fund-raising committee of the PTA. But most of us do not feel accountable to have face-to-face time alone with our mate, because we never schedule it.

Busy schedules don't automatically lead to marriage problems, but they do present a challenge that needs to be addressed. "Marital partners may find themselves disconnected from each other because they aren't spending much time together and are really leading separate lives," says Kelly Roberts, a clinical instructor and marriage and family counselor with the Oklahoma State University Human Development and Family Sciences Department. Moreover, Roberts adds, "The super-busy lifestyle can also cause husbands and wives to feel worn down and stressed, which may make them testier with each other." This is especially true if couples aren't taking care of themselves with quality sleep and good nutrition.

We have more means of communicating today than ever before, yet couples are actually more distant from one another." That, is not only because couples are spending so much time online, but because "more often than not they're communicating with each other by sending text messages instead of talking with each other over the phone or face-to-face." These electronic exchanges of bite-sized tidbits of information are definitely not the building blocks of solid relationships, she says.

In the late 1960s the divorce rate started climbing. It rose steadily for two decades until it peaked at around 50 percent in the 1980s, where it has remained since. What brought on this spike in divorces more than anything else, Dr. Craig says, is ethical and moral decline. "The ultimate threat to marriages today is not the external stressors, but what's going on internally," says Dr. Craig. Too often in our modern society, if the marriage is or becomes "too hard" or is not exactly meeting one's needs, people have no inhibitions about walking away.

Today many people will stay in a relationship only as long as they're getting more out of it than they have to put into it. "People are more focused on making themselves happy, rather than in doing what is right. They're not nearly as committed to their marital vows as people once were." When this approach to marriage is combined with life's inevitable problems, the "glue" often does not hold, Dr. Craig says. For instance, if a debilitating illness seriously affects a spouse's ability to give to the other spouse, the relationship may not survive the test. "We live in a very self-focused world. Our advertising fosters that. We're told 'You deserve a break today' and 'it's all about me.' We've forgotten to serve others—and that's what marriage is all about—'How can I meet your needs?' rather than focusing on 'What's in it for me?' Online infidelity is the epitome of this mentality: "I have my needs and nobody else is fulfilling them, so I'll just take care of myself and I'll do my own thing."

With many, religion is no longer the authority in their lives, so everything the Bible says about what a marriage should and shouldn't be like—including teachings against adultery—doesn't matter to them. There aren't any absolutes anymore in our society—no definite rights and wrongs. This secular, "no-commitment, me-first" approach to marriage got its foothold in the late 1960s and early '70s—the era of free love, drugs and antiauthority sentiment. That's also when the "no-fault" divorce revolution began, which allowed one spouse to dissolve a marriage for any reason—or for no reason at all.

Since then, there has been a growing acceptance of divorce. "It's so easy nowadays to get divorced," observes Koppe. There certainly are reasons divorce is sometimes warranted, such as in an abusive situation. But today, "more often than not, couples just grow out of love with each other and don't try to solve the problems. People don't work at marriage like they used to. They don't want to have to endure any kind of difficulties." What a contrast from God's intentions for marriage! We're told over and over again in the Bible that marriage is to be a lifelong commitment. Matthew 19:6Jesus states,

> "So they are no longer two, but one flesh. Therefore what God has joined together, let no one separate." "There is no concession for "if the marriage is no longer gratifying."

In 1 Corinthians 7:10-24 Paul addresses the problem of divorce, which was quite common during that time in cities like Corinth.

> "To the married I give this command (not I, but the Lord): A wife must not separate from her husband. But if she does, she must remain unmarried or else be reconciled to her husband. And a husband must not divorce his wife. To the rest I say this (I, not the Lord): If any brother has a wife who is not a believer and she is willing to live with him, he must not divorce her. And if a woman has a husband who is not a believer and he is willing to live with her, she must not divorce him. For the unbelieving husband has been sanctified through his wife, and the unbelieving wife has been sanctified through her believing husband. Otherwise your children would be unclean, but as it is, they are holy.

To put it in modern terms, face the difficulties and work out your differences. Ultimately, unconditional commitment is the key to successfully resisting all these marital stressors. It is only when husbands and wives are totally committed to each other that they will be able to withstand the pressures of life that are sure to come their way. That means striving to live by the standards for marriage spelled out in the Bible. This includes putting each other's needs before your own, not giving up on each other during difficulties, and working through situations together as a team. This kind of commitment is the most important step you can take to weather any kind of marital storm.

While we know stress can cause health problems ranging from chronic pain to stroke, the latest research suggests that marital stress in particular may be as destructive to your health as smoking. Even the most blissfully married couples stress each other out at times. But the key question to ask yourself: Does your relationship help or hurt your overall stress level?

"Sex relieves stress and makes you feel more energized," says sex therapist Ian Kerner, author of Love in the Time of Colic. "Couples that have regular sex feel better about their lives, better about their relationships, and they're less stressed." And while your libido may be lacking when you're under pressure, if you coax your body to go through the motions, your mind will follow. On the blog Christian Marriage Today the following information was listed.

## Reasons for Your Wife's Low Interest in Sex were listed:

### Possible Physical Reasons

**Anemia**—the word anemia means "without blood." It's an iron deficiency caused by a deficiency in red blood cells. This can only be diagnosed by a doctor but is easily treated with iron supplements and/or eating more leafy green vegetables.

**Diabetes**—a metabolism disorder characterized by abnormally high levels of glucose in the blood. In women, diabetes can cause vaginal dryness and infections that make intercourse painful.

**Hyperprolactinaemia**—an over active pituitary gland. Characterized by high levels of the hormone prolactin in the blood. In women, this can cause loss of libido, and vaginal dryness among other things.

**Possible Psychological Reasons**

**Unforgiveness**—she forgave you intellectually, but emotionally she's still stuck in the past.

**She Doesn't Feel Loved**—feeling loved is a basic human need. And if your wife's emotional needs go unmet, she may become as cold as ice towards you. Your wife must be able to feel your love as you demonstrate it daily in your words and behavior. Other emotional needs she has are: feeling valued, feeling understood, and feeling accepted.

**Loss of Attraction**—were you under the impression that your physical appearance no longer mattered to your wife? Well, you might want to renew your gym membership and visit the cologne counter at the mall. Because how you look and smell are major turn-on's or turn-off's for your wife.

**Loss of Respect and Admiration**—for women, sexual desire comes after admiration and respect. If your goal is to entertain your wife by being the constant clown, you may be shooting yourself in the foot, so to speak. A woman desires a man who she can look up to. If she doesn't look up to you, it doesn't matter how many times you bring her breakfast in bed or wash the dishes. She's not going to desire you physically.

**New Baby Obsession**—sometimes new mothers become so enthralled with their new babies that they forget about the needs of their husband. Scheduled date nights might be the answer for this problem.

**She's Burnt Out**—does your wife work both in and outside of the home? Does she plan the meals, do the laundry, attend PTA, and work a 9 to 5? Unfortunately, by the time she's done distributing pieces of herself to everyone else, she has nothing left to give you. What's the solution? Simply give her a helping hand more often with things such as dinner and picking up behind yourself. It's a win-win arrangement for both of you.

**Sexual Abuse**—if your wife was sexually abused earlier in life but never received professional help, painful memories maybe preventing her from enjoying sexual intimacy with you. Talk to her about the benefits of seeking professional help.

## Reasons for Your Husband's Low Libido

### Possible Physical Reasons

**Hyperprolactinaemia**—an over active pituitary gland. Characterized by high levels of the hormone prolactin in the blood. In men, this can cause loss of libido, and erectile dysfunction.

**Low Testosterone Levels**—after the age of thirty, it is possible for a man to lose up to two percent of testicular function every year. This correlates to low testosterone levels. Low testosterone levels can eliminate his sex drive and change his mood among other things. This condition is related to aging and is known as andropause.

**High Blood Pressure**—over a long period of time, high blood pressure damages the lining of blood vessels and can cause narrowing and hardening of the arteries. This may result in decreased blood flow to the penis and difficulty achieving and maintaining erections.

**Alcoholism and Drug Abuse**—sadly, there are many Christians who struggle with substance abuse. If your husband is a drug user, the side effects can be detrimental to his sexual health. Consider a good drug rehabilitation program.

## Possible Psychological Reasons

**Wounded Ego**—contrary to popular belief, men are emotional creatures with very fragile egos. Ladies, your man must feel that you are attracted to him, desire him, and respect him. Have you ever blasted your husband in a fit of rage, i.e., telling him how useless he is? Or, do you constantly rebel and argue with him? If so, this is likely the reason why his passion for you has diminished.

**Fear of Rejection**—If you have established a pattern of always rejecting your husband's sexual advances, he may have a fear of being rejected. After a period of time, he feels it's emotionally safer not to initiate sex than it is to risk being rejected again.

**Stress**—a decreased sex drive is a frequent complaint of those who are under constant mental stress. A study revealed that people who work more than 48 hours a week experience major problems with their sex lives. There are many techniques for reducing stress. Getting a massage, meditating, exercising, and eating healthier are all practical things your man can do to manage stress.

**Depression**—depression evokes feelings of hopelessness and helplessness. If left untreated, depression can cause a person to completely withdraw from social activities and those things they once enjoyed, like sex.

# CHAPTER XIII

## TIPS FOR MANAGING STRESS

The impact of stress and burnout on a marriage can be devastating. Here are some tips on handling stress. All too often, it's easy to react to marital stress in counterproductive ways like denial, avoidance, suppression, compromising, venting or living like roommates instead of partners.

According to several recent studies, a stressful marriage can create more health problems for someone than if they had never married at all. Another suggests that a stressful marriage can be as bad for the heart as a regular smoking habit!

To keep your marriage or long-term relationship low-stress, strong and happy, it's critical to learn to manage your attitudes and emotions and lead with your heart—from that intelligent, self-secure place inside, where wisdom, intuition and understanding reside.

"Home is the place where we're supposed to feel safe and relax from the stresses of outside life," says psychotherapist Tina Tessina, author of Money, Sex, and Kids: Stop Fighting About the Three Things That Can Ruin Your Marriage. "When there's stress at home, there's no time to recover or heal, and over time, that stress does physical damage." Here are some tips to stress-proof your marriage.

### Read Together

Set aside time each day, or at least once a week, to read the Bible together. This might also be described as a time of devotions.

### Work and Dream Together

In your walks and talks and laughter and tears, go back together, and relive the thoughts of a young boy who sat on a hillside, looking at the sky and dreaming of the future. Discuss and analyze those dreams lovingly and understandingly with one another. Then work and pray together to make them come true. In like manner, relive the hopes and aspirations of a young girl who often walked alone at sunset across her father's fields—dreaming of a husband and home of her own someday, of children, security, warmth, laughter and joy. Be sure you work together to make her dreams come true.

## Pray Together

We are not to form a covenant relationship with an unbeliever. "Do not be yoked together with unbelievers. For what do righteousness and wickedness have in common? Or what fellowship can light have with darkness? 2 Corinthians 6:14.

We should be able to pray with our spouse. Set aside times each day to pray with your spouse. Together, as a couple, bring the things that cause you stress to God in prayer. Ask Him to help you discern what to do to ease the stress in your lives and to help you stay committed to your marriage. Let Him know your needs.

## Trust in God's provision together

> Philippians 4:19 tells us "And my God will meet all your needs according to the riches of his glory in Christ Jesus."

This helps develop true intimacy with each other and with God, perhaps a better time for a couple might be just before going to bed each night. It's impossible to fall asleep angry when you've just held hands together in God's presence.

## Attend Church Together

Religious and cultural differences have been listed as a cause for divorce. Discuss your differences prior to the marriage. Marriage is complex and both partners must be willing to work on every aspect.

Get involved in a church together. Find a place of worship where you and your spouse will not only attend together, but enjoy areas of mutual interest, such as serving in a ministry and making Christian friends together. The Bible says in Hebrews 10:24-25, that one of the best ways we can stir up love and encourage good deeds is by remaining faithful to the Body of Christ by meeting together regularly as believers. We need to understand that relationships need to work together in order for the relationship to be the best it can be.

## Marriage Means Giving

After a lifetime of giving and serving, at the end of His human life, Jesus Christ gave Himself for the Church. So all husbands are instructed:

> "Husbands, love your wives, just as Christ loved the church and gave himself up for her to make her holy, cleansing her by the washing with water through the word, and to present her to himself as a radiant church, without stain or wrinkle or any other blemish, but holy and blameless. In this same way, husbands ought to love their wives as their own bodies. He who loves his wife loves himself." (Ephesians 5:25–28).

## Continue Dating

Set aside special, regular times to continue developing your romance. Once married, couples often neglect the area of romance, especially after the kids come along. Continuing a dating life may take some strategic planning on your part as a couple, but it is vital to maintaining a secure and intimate marriage. Keeping the romantic love alive will also be a bold testimony to the strength of your Christian marriage.

## Plan for couple time

Carve out time in your schedule, several times a week, to be alone with your mate and get away from whatever is causing you stress. Plan regularly scheduled date nights and weekend activities. If a getaway is not immediately possible, then make it a goal toward which you will work. Take a walk together. Go out to dinner. Have a picnic at the park. Get up a half hour earlier during the workweek so that you and your spouse can have a quiet breakfast in bed before you leave for the office. Go out for coffee Sunday morning while your teens are still asleep. Share a pot of tea after the kids are in bed."

No matter how terrible the stress is, you should give yourselves a respite now and then." If you can't fit "couple time" into your busy schedule, you need to reprioritize your time commitments so that you can. By spending time with your partner, you will be able to understand how to negotiate the problems and solve conflicts.

## Create a Spiritual Connection

It is God who ordained marriage. It is Jesus Christ, who said, "So they are no longer two, but one flesh. Therefore what God has joined together, let no one separate." Matthew 19:6.

> "But I want you to realize that the head of every man is Christ, and the head of the woman is man and the head of Christ is God. (1 Corinthians 11:3).

Every man alive has the opportunity to be the direct representative of God over his own home—in teaching, instructing, leading and inspiring his wife and children to learn and obey the words of the Holy Bible and to worship and serve the God who made them. Most wives and children will instantly and gladly respond if given half a chance! They must set a dynamic example of dedication to their Creator, study of His Word, pray to God at mealtimes—and family prayer as well as private prayer on one's knees in the bedroom, closet or other private place.

This can be achieved through an affiliation with a church, through meditation and prayer and by simply spending time in an intimate conversation. When you get closer to God you get closer to each other. Marital intimacy can open your relationship to a whole new level of enjoyment and closeness. It is important, however, to remember that intimacy does not always mean sexuality. An often forgotten aspect of intimacy is the emotional type. An example of emotional intimacy is creating a safe space for your partner to share his or her emotions without fear of you being judgmental or making light of them. Learn the difference between emotional and physical intimacy and when each one is most appropriate.

Some husbands do allow themselves to become "bitter" because their wives do not measure up to an angelic idol of perfection envisioned in their own human imaginations! But a wife was never intended to be an idol! She was never designed to be perfect in this life any more than her husband was! She was designed and created—by the Maker of us all—to be a sweetheart, help and inspiration to a man who would share himself with her, go over his plans, hopes and dreams with her, give her encouragement and guidance, and lead their home in an attitude of confidence and love! God intended the man to be the spiritual leader in the home.

The man should set an example of self-discipline in the fear of God. He should show that he is man enough—strong enough—to conquer his lusts and control his appetites. By conquering his smoking habit, by controlling his drinking and other appetites, by restraining his emotions and directing them in the right channels, by controlling and guiding his tongue according to the "law of kindness," he can set an example which will never be forgotten by his sons and daughters as they grow up. And this example will certainly command the respect, admiration and love of any sensitive, wise woman.

If couples will truly study the Bible to see what it says about marriage, if they will strive to follow the biblical teachings, principles and examples in their marriage then they will be blessed indeed. If a newly married couple would get down on their knees and sincerely seek God to lead and guide in their marriage, and then study His inspired Word and follow it, they would have a kind of "heaven on earth," at least as far as their marriage was concerned! I have seen these principles work in this way in my own marriage and in the marriages of many, many others who trusted in God. It is up to every one of us to make God the very center of our marriage!

## Show your affection

Make it a point to tell each other "I love you," and say it often. "When you are in the middle of something awful, that is the worst time to just assume your mate knows how you feel." "It's during the tough times that your partner needs the reassurance of your love even more." Cultivate a positive and thankful mind-set. We're told in 1 Thessalonians 5:18,

> "give thanks in all circumstances; for this is God's will
> for you in Christ Jesus."

No matter what the situation, there's always something to be thankful for. Learn to appreciate your spouse's good qualities—rather than dwell on his or her shortcomings. A thankful mate is pleasant to be around. Not only that, but if you maintain a positive outlook, your spouse is likely to follow suit.

## Seek counsel

In Proverbs 13:20, the Bible states the importance of seeking the advice of wise individuals.

> "Walk with the wise and become wise, for a companion
> of fools suffers harm."

If you or your mate are struggling with any of the issues discussed, be willing to get the professional help you need. Depending on the problem, this help might come from your pastor, a professional marriage and family counselor, or a financial adviser. "It's best to go to counseling as soon as you start having problems, rather than wait until they become breaking points," Roberts advises.

Look at challenges as opportunities to strengthen your marriage. The "rough spots" you and your spouse face can actually bring the two of you closer. "When you work together through it all in a constructive way—you're communicating, you're appreciating each other, you're putting each other's needs above your own—you come out stronger and close." "You'll then have confidence to face the next issue down the road." Reminding yourself of this can help you have the determination to hang in there.

We certainly live in a stressful world. Our lives are full of challenges. What's important is that you and your husband or wife support each other during the tough times, rather than allow life's difficulties to pull you apart! These steps require real, committed effort on your part. Falling in love may have seemed effortless, but keeping your Christian marriage strong will take ongoing work. The good news is—building a healthy marriage is not all that complicated or difficult if you're determined to follow a few basic principles.

### Be Attractive

Like many men, your man is visually stimulated. When he sees you looking sweet and sexy, he's going to want some play time. It doesn't matter if the two of you just had a heated argument. So, take a moment to do a self-inventory. Have you put on extra weight? Are you always wearing sweats and sneakers? Do you purposely make yourself look good for your husband? Or, have you let yourself go? Perhaps it's time you made a few adjustments.

### Start cuddling

If sex isn't an option, cuddle up on the couch instead. Studies show that couples who spend more time hugging and kissing have lower levels of stress hormones in their bodies. For one week, researchers from the University of Zurich in Switzerland studied 51 couples who were either married or living together and found that those who reported more physical contact—from holding hands to having sex—had lower levels of the stress hormone cortisol in their saliva.

## Work together as a team

When you have different opinions, don't focus on who's right or wrong. Instead, focus on what will work," says Tessina. Successful couples try to solve the problem by identifying it, brainstorming ideas, and coming up with a solution—together. Once you have a plan, outline how it will take shape and who's responsible for what.

## Prioritize your relationship

When you have kids, relationship satisfaction usually starts to decline. You have to be dependable, responsible, and scheduled—and routine can kill sexual attraction. To reconnect, make sure you have a regular date night and find ways to bring newness into your lives. "Protecting your marriage should be at the top of your priority list as a parent," says Kerner. "It's important to your child's well-being to see that his parents are happy and connected."

## Show gratitude

Research shows that it's important to hear five positive statements for every negative one from your partner. Clearly, you're not going to keep a careful count. But you can show gratitude for everything your partner does to hold up his end. "Happy couples know how to express their gratitude and appreciation. They celebrate their love."

## Tune in

Listening is critical to reducing stress in a marriage. "A big percentage of arguments are caused by getting louder in a futile effort to be heard." Instead of duking it out with your vocal cords, allow each person uninterrupted talk time. Try setting a timer for three minutes to start. Then paraphrase what your partner said to make sure you heard it correctly.

## Take some time off

Sure, you spend most of your downtime with your partner and kids, but it's important to get solo time (or time with your girlfriends). "Couples need to do things apart that they can talk about later," says Tessina. It refreshes the relationship and helps you miss each other a bit, too.

## Have fun

Make sure you do things as a couple that don't involve paying bills, cleaning house, and raising the kids. "Doing something together that you enjoy gives you shared experiences and reminds you that life isn't all about responsibility," says Kerner. Go for a hike, take a dance class, or hit the tennis court with your partner, and you'll get an exercise boost to boot.

## Set it aside

Once again the issue about cell phones; it should go without saying that cell phones are best kept out of sight and out of mind when you're on a date. Turn it off and place it in your bag or pocket for the duration—the world won't end if you can't check your e-mail for an hour or two. I also recommend shutting tablets, phones and laptops at night, or at least charging them in a room other than your bedroom. Not only can they interfere with your ability to relax and unwind, but their distracting presence can also put a real crimp in intimacy. Don't let stress sabotage your relationship, says Thomas Bradbury, co-founder of the UCLA Relationship Institute. His advice:

## Get stress on your radar

Learn to recognize when your partner is feeling stressed, and cut him or her some slack.

## Step up

When your partner is tired and stressed, that's your signal to step up and do more around the house, Bradbury says. "But if you complain about helping, you are making your partner feel worse, not better."

## Build a firewall

Partners in healthy relationships know how to prevent ordinary frustrations from spilling over to erode the good feelings that they have for one another. "So build a firewall around all of the great things you and your partner share, and protect them against minor annoyances."

## Strengthen the foundation

Good relationships are fundamentally about two people taking care of each other. Figure out what your partner needs to feel secure and happy and do your best to give it to them.

## Get active

If stress is eating away at your relationship, get on your feet and invite your partner to a walk, a class or a movie. Some researchers, such as McNulty, have focused on a subject such as forgiveness, while others examine conflict or commitment. As stress has increased in our daily lives, there's particularly strong interest now in how partner interactions over the first year chart the course for the relationship. A low level of marital happiness is not the only predictor of divorce; happy marriages may also end in divorce due to stressful life events, low commitment and negative communication.

Margaret Wheeler Johnson suggests more Ways To Keep Stress From Hurting Your Marriage.

- Work the important stuff out before you get married (to the extent that you can).
- If you have trouble coping with stress, marry someone who is less affected by it.
- Know that your job affects your marriage.
- Have a plan and Reevaluate the plan.
- Even if you think you're doing everything right, reevaluate the plan.
- Choose sex over your to-do list.

- Do not underestimate the power of exercise (and kale).
- Forget other people's expectations, or "We're just happier. Deal with that."
- If they aren't too devastating, the hard times make you stronger.

Most of University of Texas psychologist Lisa Neff's work on stress and marriage shows that the best way to keep stress from weakening relationships is to cut out as many stressors as possible. That said, two studies she conducted in 2011 showed that couples who had good coping skills and were exposed to mild to moderate stress as newlyweds were more resilient in the face of later stressors, including parenthood, than those who had good coping skills but saw relatively little stress during the early phases of matrimony.

There's no denying the fact that motherhood is stressful: According to a recent TODAY Moms survey, moms on average say their stress level is 8.5 . . . Managing marriage stress starts with self, figure out what is bothering you. Stress is tricky. We often say "I'm so stressed out!" but may have trouble figuring out what is causing it. Take the time to find out what the problem is and then share it with your spouse. Your partner may be able to help you deal with your stress. With increased awareness of what you are worried about, he/she can think of ways to keep from adding to your stress. The Female Stress Syndrome Survival Guide by Georgia Witkin, Ph.D. is an excellent resource.

Bear in mind that your partner may not think you have any reason to be stressed. Help him/her understand why you are. Respect each other's values and find ways to work together on the challenges. Your partner can give you a different point of view and together you can brainstorm ways to solve the issue that is causing your stress. Recognize that not every problem (or stressor) has a solution, but talking about it and sharing your feelings can help you manage it. Understand that if you don't figure out how to successfully handle stress with your partner, problems in your marriage may emerge.

## Stay Connected

Sometimes couples spend more time talking with their friends than their spouses about issues because they feel their partner might not understand them. Turning away from your partner during stressful events can be one of the most damaging behaviors in a relationship. This can lead to feelings of rejection. Silence leads to greater frustration and increased anger, which can drive the two of you apart.

Try to strengthen your relationship by turning to each other often. You can do this by simply talking about the every-day events that happen in your lives, like the news, a good movie you saw, or the accomplishments of your children. This builds the confidence and trust you both need so you can discuss heavier and potentially stressful topics when they arise.

## Maintain Intimacy

Intimacy is an important part of any successful marriage. While many people think intimacy pertains only to sex, it is much more than that. Being intimate with your partner means that you reveal your thoughts and your feelings (even though it may be embarrassing to do so), demonstrate affection, and work together to solve problems. By being open and honest we develop emotional intimacy. When we are stressed this is especially important. Intimacy gives your partner a chance to support you and in return, you are more likely to support them when they are stressed. Couples might avoid becoming intimate with their partner during stressful times because they are too tired or emotionally drained, but this can be a mistake. Being intimate actually helps relieve tension and anxiety.

## Find Balance

You can become overwhelmed with activities that you really don't have time for causing problems in your relationship and with the entire family. The more time spent on other things, the less time there is for the family. Research has shown that work stress is linked to unhappiness in marriage. Don't be a workaholic by choosing to stay connected through cell phones, emails and other technology. This can cause your partner to feel lonely and will hurt your relationship. Parents can feel like keeping up with each family member's schedule is a full time job. Scheduling the children's activities and taking them to practices, games, recitals and events can get to be too much. To avoid family burn-out keep an eye out for signs of stress and cut back on activities as needed.

If you are feeling overwhelmed and don't know how to get back on track to a healthy marriage, it is a good idea to take a relationship education course. It can give you the skills and resources you need to help manage stress and make your relationship better.

The kind of spouse, parent, or friend you are is shown by your actions and attitudes. Be watchful of long periods of loneliness, depression or mood swings in yourself or in your partner. If you see these signs, be willing to help or get help. Try to be aware of each other's emotions every day. Change the things in your life, or in your relationship, that you can control and accept the things that you cannot change.

Stress can come in many forms. The one thing you can count on is that it will be in your life. Try to remember that everyone handles stress differently. In other words, what causes one person to "stress-out" may be something that another person can easily handle. We have a choice about how we react to stress. You and your spouse can together make an effort to control your thoughts and behaviors. Choose to lessen the effects of stress by communicating with each other to keep each other from feeling lonely. Build trust, show commitment and release the heavy burdens that you are feeling. Be kind, caring and show affection.

# CHAPTER XIV

## MARRIAGE AND MINISTRY

These times present many challenges for marriages, ministries and marriages in ministry. Everything that I have researched and I have included about marriage applies to all marriages even marriages in ministry. In addition I have included this chapter specifically for Ministry marriages. The Christian Reformed Church in N.A. from Michigan has prepared a resource tool for Ministries through their Sustaining Pastoral Excellence Program. It is titled Marriage and Ministry and is an excellent resource and an excellent training tool for Pastors and Church Boards. The following recommendations are addressed to ministry marriages.

**Sabbath Rest:**

If we do not regularly quit work for one day a week, we take ourselves far too seriously. Sabbath strengthens marriages and energizes ministries. Sabbath involves quiet reflection, sharing, family time, and prayer. Sabbath rejuvenates. Sabbath refocuses. Sabbath re-roots. Set aside one day of each week for Sabbath rest.
- Determine what you will do on your Sabbath day and what it will look like.
- Commit to keeping the day each week.
- Ensure accountability to your council for taking Sabbath rest by sharing how it benefits you and your ministry.

**Peer Groups**

Peer group involvement has the capacity to strengthen both ministry and marriage. You can open up about pastoral challenges. Spouses can become actively involved in the group—bringing their perspectives to the table. Together as pastor couples, you are able to explore each other's hearts and minds and allow the Holy Spirit to do the same. Share thoughts and feelings, divulge weaknesses and shortcomings encourage growth, offer prayers, and ask for blessings to strengthen the work in the church.

Peer group involvement has the capacity to strengthen both ministry and marriage. Peer groups come in many different shapes and sizes. Some are theologically-oriented, while others focus on emotional support. Build skills for ministry while providing a place for sharing and fellowship. The Spirit of God truly works with pastors and spouses to accomplish objectives. It is a safe place to unwind and to share honestly and openly.

- Talk to your spouse about peer group involvement and its many benefits.
- Commit to joining—or starting—a peer group in your region.

**Sabbatical**: (An extended, planned, intentional time away for the purpose of personal renewal and re-energizing).

Sabbaticals are an important part of nurturing healthy marriage and ministry. A sabbatical helps prevent burnout by providing time for renewal of mind and body—including physical renewal (eating properly and getting regular exercise), mental renewal (taking a college or seminary class, either audited or for credit), and spiritual renewal (spending time in solitude, retreat, and reflection).

A sabbatical can play a major role in preventing burnout when it helps a pastor balance these physical, mental, and spiritual needs. A sabbatical contributes to marital renewal by providing extended time for relaxation, renewal, and time away from the center of the church. This supports and nurtures healthy marriage and family relationships, allowing a pastor to return from sabbatical refreshed and re-energized for the work of ministry.

## Relationships

God made us social beings and instilled in us a need for friendship. Pastors and their spouses are no exception. Pastors spend countless hours listening to, counseling, teaching, and helping others. Being able to clearly distinguish pastoral relationships from friendships is important for the health of a pastor, spouse, and family. Some pastor couples find friendships within their own church. Sometimes this works, but it can also present significant challenges. Many pastors seek out friendships from the broader community or from other congregations.

Another possible source of friendships for pastor couples may be individuals who have served in ministry in the past or individuals who have lived in a pastor's family. People with a ministry background often have a better understanding of the special challenges pastors and their families face. They are also sensitive to the high level of confidentiality required in ministry. Another option is for pastor couples to seek out friendships with other pastor couples, either from the same denomination or a different one.

## Council Retreats:

Churches should consider planning retreats that allow pastor and council members to get to know each other on a personal level, as Jesus knew his disciples. Planning a Retreat: Your retreat plan should include but not be limited to:

- a written plan outlining how you will spend your time;
- an offsite location for overnight accommodations
- time for prayer and sharing of scripture passages
- an opportunity for individuals to be paired with someone they do not know very well
- time for worship and praise
- time for individual reflection, meditation, and prayer
- celebration of the Lord's Supper

**Retreats and Seminars:**

Retreats have value for pastor, spouse, and church. Pastor retreats are a place to let go and regroup; they are essential for marriage and ministry. A seminar is an educational forum, a place for study and discussion. Seminars help pastors do important maintenance and upgrades. Retreats are focused on spiritual wellness, emotional completeness, and nurturing healthy marriage relationships. Churches directly benefit when their pastor and/or pastor couple spend time on retreat. Prayer and time to relax help keep a pastor energized to serve.

A seminar is an educational forum, a place for study and discussion. Like the tools a tradesperson relies upon, seminars help pastors do important maintenance and upgrades. At seminars, pastors sharpen their ministry skills, expand their ministry horizons, and renew their lives for service in the church. The entire church benefits when a pastor attends seminars that teach, challenge, and equip for service.

While many seminars are geared to the pastor, some are designed for the pastor couple. Since spouses play such an important role in the church's ministry, they should be included in these learning events whenever possible. Understanding the changing nature of ministry dynamics is important not only for the pastor but for the spouse as well.

**Intentional Reflection**: (A habit that involves speaking with others about the important things of life and ministry in a deliberate and planned way).

It is intended to allow the pastor couple to examine their experiences of ministry in light of their goals for learning, growth, and spiritual formation. Often, a pastor and his or her spouse and family are at serious risk for not having their spiritual, pastoral, and relationship needs met. For this reason, it is important for them to engage in intentional reflection. Intentional reflection can be carried out in many different settings, but it is intended to allow the pastor couple to examine their experiences of ministry in light of their goals for learning, growth, and spiritual formation. Intentional reflection involves the sharing of thoughts and feelings, a kind of honest and open communication that exposes personal vulnerabilities.

Ministry is all about relationships, and intentional reflection involves strengthening the family relationships that support ministry. Worshipping together as a family contributes to the spiritual well-being of the family unit and therefore it is important for a pastor's family to find opportunities to worship together regularly.

**Pastor-Church Relations Committee** (Providing pastoral care for the physical, social, and spiritual life of the pastor's family is essential for the pastor's marriage and ministry).

This team regularly checks in on and takes care to ensure that the family's physical and spiritual needs are being met. By meeting regularly and dealing with issues as they arise, a PCR committee helps ensure that the pastor couple is not carrying their burdens alone.

**Balance:**

How might a better balance be achieved so that ministry does not outweigh a pastor's marriage?

A weekly day off to spend time with spouse, pay the bills, get the car repaired, work on projects and/or hobbies, work out at the gym, or give attention to personal finances.

Pastors need annual vacations to relax and enjoy God's beautiful world and revel in the gift of family and friends.

Monthly date nights provide an opportunity for a pastor couple to strengthen their marriage relationship.

Pastor's Action Plan
- Take care of yourself, your spouse, and your marriage.
- Take a regularly scheduled day off each week.

- Take your full vacation each year.
- Plan monthly date nights.
- Strive for a healthy balance between marriage and ministry.
- Share your challenges in achieving balance with your spouse and council.

**Boundaries and Expectations:**

Establishing and encouraging clear boundaries between church and home is crucial for the health of marriage and ministry. One important part of this encouragement is to hold a pastor accountable for taking full annual vacation and other time off work and to fully release the pastor from duties during these times. Maintaining office space outside the family home as well as separate phone lines for church and home helps establish clear boundaries.

Often, churches have unfair expectations of a pastor's family. Expectations regarding a pastor's spouse and the children can also create challenges for marriage and ministry. Allow them the freedom to become who God wants them to be. Essential to the health of a pastor's marriage and ministry is a Covenant of agreement regarding expectations. It should include: hours of work; time off and annual vacation; Sabbatical; Professional Development, retreats and seminars and compensation.

Pastor's Action Plan

- Establish clear boundaries between home and church.
- Seek support from professional peers outside the church.
- Take care of your marriage and your children.
- Insist that your church develop a Covenant of Agreement to clearly define expectations.

**Burnout**: (a decreased level of motivation to do tasks that were once very fulfilling.).

Unrealistic expectations by the pastors themselves or sometimes by the congregation of their pastor or failing to overcome obstacles caused by interpersonal conflict in the church or the home lead to burnout. Churches can help best by reaching out with love, support, and encouragement. Random acts of kindness can help restore a pastor's hope and vision. A Healthy habit: let go and let God.

A key ingredient in preventing burnout is to build up the things that make for a happy and healthy marriage. A pastor with a positive and nurturing marriage and family life will have greater vitality for ministry. Churches also need to ensure that a pastor has enough time to spend with his or her children. If the demands of the church leave little or no time for family needs, burnout is on the horizon.

Pastor's Action Plan

- Become aware of the symptoms of burnout.
- Have realistic expectations of your skills and time.
- Ask for help when needed.
- Develop healthy work habits.

**Balancing Marriage & Ministry; Family matters**

Why does it happen? How does it happen? How can you prevent it from happening to you? And why do we feel like we need to work so long and hard?

Get your family together and craft a family mission statement. It's just as important to be intentional as a family as it is to do so where you work. We wanted our family to be on the same page as to why we were here on earth and what principles would govern our time together; we wanted a grid for decision making and conflict to pass through.

**Carve out time for your family each week** . . . in advance.
Put it on your calendar. Stop saying you have got to get "one more thing done" before you leave for home. Plan your week with specific

ending times and stick to them.

**Eliminate things from your schedule that aren't important.**

March to the mission that Jesus called you to, not the mission that others want you to do for them. Be ruthless here!

**If your work situation requires constant excessive hours** to get the job done, it's time to evaluate other ways to accomplish the task.

Pray for the Lord to send workers into your harvest field and then sit back and watch them go to work. Pray for supernatural results from the time you do put into your day, then go home and be a minister to the other mission field God gave you . . . your family.

If you're a leader of others, have people actually write into their job descriptions the need to be committed to their family and specifically how they will do this.

Develop an activity with your family as a whole and or with individual family members; maybe its hiking, a date at Denny's for breakfast on Saturday or coffee with your spouse where you pray together for your day. As you do this, remember that those teachable moments are almost like intentional accidents, they happen, but not always because you planned them. So be sure to plan large quantities of time throughout the year so they'll have a chance to occur.

Create a spiritual life development plan for each of your kids outlining their strengths, their areas for improvement and your plans to shape their character as they grow up under your care. Our children are arrows that are being sent to a world that we will never fully see. It's our job to shape them into arrows that will fly straight and travel the distance to the Kingdom target that God has intended for them.

Schedule a date night of at least an hour once a week with each child or your spouse where you just focus on them. It doesn't have to be expensive; time alone is the critical ingredient here. When the budget is tight, have this time in your back yard with your son.

When you're traveling, send e-mail or a postcard back to your family.

Call them on the phone and pray with them in addition to chatting.

At the end of a day, ask your kids or spouse these three questions . . .

"What happened today that you're proud of?"

"What happened today that you wish you could do over?" "Where did you see God in your day today?"

If your children were asked to call out words today that defined your parenting, or if your spouse was reviewing your life at your funeral service, what words would they use? Many words that are called out today to define their father are negative words. Words like "absent," "domineering" and "detached." If you're not happy with what words are echoing around in your head, it's time to make some changes in how you're leading your family. And by the way, if you're the man in your family, make sure you're not abdicating all the work of leading your family to your wife; the role of leadership is not designed to be shouldered solely by her. Get involved! I love how Eugene Petersen in The Message puts it, "Exploit or abuse your family, and end up with a fistful of air . . .

"Whoever brings ruin on their family will inherit only wind, and the fool will be servant to the wise." (Proverbs 11:29).

Are you pleased with the investment you have made in building your family and your marriage so far? If the answer is no, why not make a few important dates with your kids and your spouse now. Pastors are you avoiding common pitfalls?

**Quality counselors will not allow pastors to engage in these practices.**

**First**, you must not focus your attention on your spouse's faults. You can only change yourself and must focus here.

**Second**, you must reject spousal accusations because they are only partially true. The slightest exaggeration of your flaws in a spousal accusation mobilizes your defenses against it, even if most of what your spouse says is true.

**Third**, you must not allow your shame to control your reactions. If you do, you will refuse the truth because you already feel so badly about yourself.

**Fourth**, you must realize that childhood trauma intensifies present-day conflict.

**Fifth**, you must acknowledge that your arrested development causes you to react by fleeing, fighting, and freezing emotionally.

**Sixth**, you must not approach relationships from a hierarchical perspective. This causes you to react on the fruitless level of I'm right and she's wrong; or husbands shouldn't have to do this and wives must do that. Instead of using this controlling destructive approach, you need to move beyond rigid roles and rules to a more godly and helpful relationship approach.

Throw away the shoulds and oughts and ask: How can I change, be more honest, more helpful? How can I give more grace? What can I do to solve the conflict? How is she experiencing me? Who can help me see how I hurt my spouse? Shift your relationship paradigms to engage in this more productive approach.

To switch patterns, change from the inside out. Start practicing more graceful approaches with your spouse. To reignite a vibrant relationship with the Lord will require skilled outside help. You and your marriage are worth it. You can always find reasons to hope. Whether your spouse wants help or wants you to reach for help, I urge you to do so today. Wives usually reach first, but men may surely take the lead.

"Always remember that God doesn't need you, your gifts or your ministry. If He did, why did He create you so late in history? Cultivate your marriage behind closed doors.

I pray you will prayerfully consider these points, examine your marriage and ask the Lord to show you anything that you may or may not be doing that needs to be corrected in the present and future.

# EPILOGUE

In 2009, the divorce rate for the United States—at 3.5 per 1000 population, was almost half the marriage rate for the nation—at 6.8 per 1000 population—which implied that almost half of the married couples in the U.S. eventually ended up getting divorced. Divorce statistics also reveal that the probability of a couple getting divorced within 10 years of marriage was a whopping 33 percent, and within 5 years was around 20 percent. So why do marriages fail? Reasons exist in plenty—right from cheating spouse to rearing of children.

We need to take a serious look at the causes of divorce and take a proactive stance. We need to do more counseling of the youth before they even get into a relationship. I pray this publication of "Marriage, God's Way" will be a resource that counselors, Pastors and couples will include in their libraries and use it for the Ministry of Marriage. We need to practice prevention rather than correction after the fact.

God created marriage for the human race. Marriage was designed to provide love, intimacy, recreation, fellowship, and procreation. You will find a surprisingly high number of people who are still very much in love with their long-term partners. Romantic love can endure. The key to keeping the romance alive is hard work by both partners and keeping God as the center of the relationship. After all my research I have found that couples who spend time together and really work and care about the relationship seem to be able to resolve conflicts relatively smoothly. Dr. Charles Swindoll says, "Marriage is the foundation of family life, and marriage is one of God's greatest tools for ministry. Our goal isn't to build stronger marriages. It's to build stronger marriages for a purpose—ministry."

The purpose is so that when others see how we interact with each other in ways that display the love of God, it could very well attract them to our lives, our homes, and ultimately to want to know our God better. And isn't that the point of the ministry that God has called you to?

> **"1 Corinthians 13:4-8.** Love is patient, love is kind. It does not envy, it does not boast, it is not proud. It does not dishonor others, it is not self-seeking, it is not easily angered, it keeps no record of wrongs. Love does not delight in evil but rejoices with the truth. It always protects, always trusts, always hopes, always perseveres. Love never fails. But where there are prophecies, they will cease; where there are tongues, they will be stilled; where there is knowledge, it will pass away.

It takes hard work to keep love alive in a marriage but it is not impossible. Your marriage is a covenant, a solemn and binding relationship which is meant to last a life time. Your life and your marriage are gifts from God, blessings from God. The love of God, the faithfulness of God, and the desire to be pleasing to God are the blessings of a godly marriage. Couples need to celebrate these blessings and give thanks. All things are possible with the joy of Christ and through Christ. Place God at the center of your marriage and your life. His love is infinite and He desires for your marriage to be a reflection of His love.

# STATISTICS ABOUT PASTORS

Pastors today are faced with more work, more problems, and more stress than any other time in the history of the church. This is taking a frightening toll on the ministry, shown by the statistics below:

**Pastors:**

- Fifteen hundred pastors leave the ministry each month due to moral failure, spiritual burnout or contention in their churches.
- Four thousand new churches begin each year, but over seven thousand churches close.
- Fifty percent of pastors' marriages will end in divorce.
- Eighty percent of pastors and eighty-four percent of their spouses feel unqualified and discouraged in their role as pastors.
- Fifty percent of pastors are so discouraged that they would leave the ministry if they could, but have no other way of making a living.
- Eighty percent of seminary and Bible school graduates who enter the ministry will leave the ministry within the first five years. Ninety percent of pastors said their seminary or Bible school training did only a fair to poor job preparing them for ministry.
- Eighty-five percent of pastors said their greatest problem is they are sick and tired of dealing with problem people, such as disgruntled elders, deacons, worship leaders, worship teams, board members, and associate pastors. Ninety percent said the hardest thing about ministry is dealing with uncooperative people.
- Seventy percent of pastors feel grossly underpaid.

- Ninety percent said the ministry was completely different than what they thought it would be before they entered the ministry.
- Seventy percent felt God called them to pastoral ministry before their ministry began, but after three years of ministry, only fifty percent still felt called.

**Pastors' Wives:**

- Eighty percent of pastors' spouses feel their spouse is overworked.
- Eighty percent of pastor' wives feel left out and unappreciated by the church members.
- Eighty percent of pastors' spouses wish their spouse would choose another profession.
- Eighty percent of pastors' wives feel pressured to do things and be something in the church that they are really not.
- The majority of pastor's wives surveyed said that the most destructive event that has occurred in their marriage and family was the day they entered the ministry.

**Pastors' Marriages:**

- Seventy percent of pastors constantly fight depression.
- Almost forty percent polled said they have had an extra-marital affair since beginning their ministry.

**Pastors' Children:**

- Eighty percent of adult children of pastors surveyed have had to seek professional help for depression.

**Pastors' Relationship With the Lord:**

- Seventy percent of pastors do not have a close friend, confidant, or mentor.

- Ninety-five percent of pastors do not regularly pray with their spouses.
- Eighty percent of pastors surveyed spend less than fifteen minutes a day in prayer.
- Seventy percent said the only time they spend studying the Word is when they are preparing their sermons.

## Divorce Among Adults Who Have Been Married

### (Base: 3792 adults)

| Population Segment | Have Been Divorced | No. of Interviews |
|---|---|---|
| **All adults** | **33%** | **3792** |
| Evangelical Christians | 26% | 339 |
| Non-evangelical born again Christians | 33% | 1373 |
| Notional Christians | 33% | 1488 |
| Associated with non Christian faith | 38% | 197 |
| Atheist or agnostic | 30% | 269 |
| All born again Christians | 32% | 1712 |
| All non born again Christians | 33% | 2080 |
| Protestant | 34% | 1997 |
| Catholic | 28% | 875 |
| Upscale | 22% | 450 |
| Downscale | 39% | 367 |
| White | 32% | 2641 |
| African-American | 36% | 464 |
| Hispanic | 31% | 458 |
| Asian | 20% | 128 |
| Conservative | 28% | 1343 |
| Moderate | 33% | 1720 |
| Liberal | 37% | 474 |

(Source: The Barna Group, Ventura, CA)

# PERSONAL MARRIAGE ASSESSMENT

## IS YOUR MARRIAGE SUCCESSFUL?

### Take the assessment and find out!

Directions: Read each statement and circle the answer that best describes your marriage.

1A. We approach our life together as a team.
    1) Always  2) Mostly  3) Sometimes  4) Never

1B. We know how to tackle a project together and successfully complete it.
    1) Always  2) Mostly  3) Sometimes  4) Never

2A. My spouse is very gifted and uses his/her gifts to enrich our family.
    1) Always  2) Mostly  3) Sometimes  4) Never

2B. My spouse is very aware of my gifts and encourages me to use them to enrich our family.
    1) Always  2) Mostly  3) Sometimes  4) Never

3A. Marriage brings out the best in me.
    1) Always  2) Mostly  3) Sometimes  4) Never

3B. I can look back on my marriage and see how, through it, I have become a better person.
    1) Always  2) Mostly  3) Sometimes  4) Never

4A. I am satisfied that we have the money we need to live the life-style we want to live.
    1) Always  2) Mostly  3) Sometimes  4) Never

4B. We agree on our approach to money, how we are to save, spend, and give a portion of it to charity.
    1) Always   2) Mostly   3) Sometimes   4) Never

5A. We are committed to and work at living a healthy lifestyle including nurturing a spiritual life.
    1) Always   2) Mostly   3) Sometimes   4) Never

5B. We have a healthy balance of work, leisure time, diet, exercise, spirituality, and sleep.
    1) Always   2) Mostly   3) Sometimes   4) Never

6A. My relationships at work (or home for the homemaker) are very positive and productive.
    1) Always   2) Mostly   3) Sometimes   4) Never

6B. I am confident at what I do, and receive affirmation and encouragement for it.
    1) Always   2) Mostly   3) Sometimes   4) Never

7A. My spouse takes good care of me when I am not feeling well.
    1) Always   2) Mostly   3) Sometimes   4) Never

7B. My spouse is the first person that I turn to for care when I am not feeling well.
    1) Always   2) Mostly   3) Sometimes   4) Never

8A. It is very important to us to be a good neighbor and pay attention to what is going on in the community.
    1) Always   2) Mostly   3) Sometimes   4) Never

8B. We are active in helping our neighborhood and community become a better place to live.
    1) Always   2) Mostly   3) Sometimes   4) Never

9A. My spouse and I are good friends and have fun going through life together.
    1) Always   2) Mostly   3) Sometimes   4) Never

9B. We regularly make time for fun and leisure activities that we do together.
  1) Always 2) Mostly 3) Sometimes 4) Never

10A. For those with children: Our children wonderfully enrich our marriage.
  1) Always 2) Mostly 3) Sometimes 4) Never

10B. For those with children: Parenthood has brought us closer together.
  1) Always 2) Mostly 3) Sometimes 4) Never

11A. We have little stress in our lives. We exercise, eat right, and make time for spirituality.
  1) Always 2) Mostly 3) Sometimes 4) Never

11B. We are very good at dealing with conflict and dealing with difficult issues.
  1) Always 2) Mostly 3) Sometimes 4) Never

12A. I am satisfied with our sexual life and find it pleasurable, meaningful, and frequent enough.
  1) Always 2) Mostly 3) Sometimes 4) Never

12B. As we get older we are able to speak with each other about our changing needs related to sex.
  1) Always 2) Mostly 3) Sometimes 4) Never


Tally your score.

Count the number of 1s, 2s, 3s, and 4s you circled. Write down each tally, then multiply that number by the indicated factor (e.g. If you had eight 1s, the score would be 8 x 1 = 8. If you had eight 2s, the score would be 8 x 2 = 16). Add the sums together to determine your total score. The lower the score, the more successful the marriage.

Your score:

Number of 1s: _____ x 1 = _____
Number of 2s: _____ x 2 = _____
Number of 3s: _____ x 3 = _____
Number of 4s: _____ x 4 = _____
Total = _____

Your results?
With children:24 -37 = Very Successful Marriage
38 -61 = Successful Marriage
62 -86 = Marriage Needs Attention
87 or greater = HELP!
Without children:22 -33 = Very Successful Marriage
34 -55 = Successful Marriage
56 -76 = Marriage Needs Attention
77 or greater = HELP!

*This marriage assessment is used with permission from Lori and Robert Fontana, directors of Catholic Life Ministries (CLM), Seattle, Washington. For more information about the Fontanas and their ministry go to catholiclifeministries.org or workonyourmarriage.org.*

# NOTES

**Introduction**

1. Larry Wood. Satan's Attack on Marriage, *Bible Doctrine News, Divine*. January 4, 1999-Revised August 2, 2010; http://www.biblenews1.com/marevil/marevil1.htm.

2. Jake & Melissa Kircher, Blip.tv. 99 Thoughts on Marriage and Ministry. Comment posted February 12, 2013.

3. *The Amplified Bible*. Grand Rapids, Michigan. Zondervan. 1987

4. D. L. Fennell. Characteristics of Long Term Marriages. *Journal of Mental Health counseling*,15 (1993); 446-60.

5. Richard H. Murphy. Statistics about Pastors. www.maranathalife.com

6. "Tips for Youth Pastors-Balancing Act-Youth Ministry". http://www.teensundayschool.com/.

**Chapter One: God's Purpose for Marriage**

1. Dr. Gary Chapman. The Marriage You've Always Wanted.

2. J. Lee Jagers. God's Purpose for Marriage: A Biblical View.

3. Dr. David Foster. God's Design for Marriage. www.focusonthefamily.com/marriage

4. Gary Thomas, Sacred Marriage. Grand Rapids, MI. Zondervan, 2000.

5. Aryeh Pamensky, Rabbi. The Purpose of Marriage. http://aish.com/family/marriage.

6. Rb Bradley. "What is God's Primary Purpose for Marriage?" Help For the Struggling Marriage. Family Ministries.com. http://www.familyministries.com/marriage_purpose.htm.

**Chapter II: Foundation Builders in Marriage**

1. How to Build a Rock Solid Foundation." http://www.inspiredabundance.com/abundance-prosperity/relationship-tips-how-to-build-a-rock-solid-foundation/.

2. Paul Chappell. "Marriage in the Ministry." http://www.paulchappell.com/2007/02/12/marriage-in-the-ministry/. Feb. 12,2007.

3. In Our Opinion. Rescuing the Family. "Deseret News. Feb. 17, 2013. http://www.deseretnews.com/article/765622761/Rescuing-the-family.html?pg=all

4. V.L. Hamlin. "How to Keep Your Marriage Strong and Healthy." Yahoo!ContributorNetwork. http://voices.yahoo.com/how-keep-marriage-strong-healthy-463580.html?cat=41.

5. John Gottman, Ph.D., Nan Silver. Seven Principles for Making Marriage Work. http://www.sacmarriageprep.com/.

6. http://www.twoofus.org/educational-content/articles/10-simple-ways-to-make-a-marriage-last/index.aspx.

7. Dave Earley. 14 Secrets to a Better Marriage. Uhrichsville, Barbour Publishing, Inc. 2011. p.14.

8. Life Success Coach Warren. "How to Build `a Rock Solid Foundation". Inspired Abundance. http://www.inspiredabundance.com/abundance-prosperity/relationship-tips-how-to-build-a-rock-solid-foundation/.

9. Tiffany Perkins Munn. "How to Ignite the Romance." http://ezinearticles.com/?How-to-%28Re%29Ignite-the-Romance-In-Your-Relationship&id=6375332.

10. Dr. Gary Chapman. The Five Love Languages. Pp20-24.

11. Dr. Vernon McGee. http://www.crosswalk.com/family/marriage/loving-your-spouse-with-a-whole-heart-11602176.html.

12. M.J. Schrader, "Why is Love so Difficult for Some People?" http://ezinearticles.com/?Why-Is-Love-Is-Difficult-for-Some-People?&id=6186743.

**Chapter III: Simple Ways to Make Marriage Last**

1. Dr. Gary Smalley. http://christianbooknotes.com/2012/interview-dr-gary-smalley/.

2. "Simple Ways to Make a Marriage Last." http://jtfstraighttalk.blogspot.com/2010/06/10-simple-ways-to-make-marriage-last.html. June 10, 2010.

3. Pat Strawbridge. "The Adventure of a Successful Marriage." http://ezinearticles.com/?The-Adventure-of-a-Successful-Marriage&id=259033.

4. Stuart Wolpert. "Here is What Real Commitment to your Marriage Means." http://www.eurekalert.org/pub_releases/2012-02/uoc--hiw020112.php. Feb.1,2012.

**Chapter IV Know Each Other**

1. Roderick Meredith. "God's Plan for a Happy Marriage." http://www.tomorrowsworld.org/booklets/gods-plan-for-happy-marriage.

## Chapter V: How to Communicate in Your Marriage

1. Abhijit Naik. Buzzle: Published Nov. 19, 2010.
   http://www.buzzle.com/articles/top-reasons-for-divorce-in-america.html.

2. Barry & Mary Leventhal. Two Becoming One. The Art of Marital Communication—Christian Marriage Help.
   http://www.crosswalk.com/family/marriage/the-art-of-marital-communication-1193737.html.

3. Joe Beam. How to Communicate in Your Marriage. Love Path International. Jan. 14, 2011.
   http://www.crosswalk.com/family/marriage/how-to-communicate-in-your-marriage-11644209.html?p=2

4. Dennis Rainey. The Number One Problem in Marriage-Family
   http://www.familylife.com/articles/topics/marriage/staying-married/communication/the-number-one-problem-in-marriage#.U7LJHbG9aC8.

## Chapter VI: Conflict Resolution

1. Willard F. Harley Jr. His Needs Her Needs. Grand Rapids, Michigan. Fleming H. Revell 2004.p.15

2. Sheri & Bob Stritof. How to Fight Fair in Marriage.
   http://marriage.about.com/cs/conflictanddanger/ht/fightfair.html.

3. Guidelines for Resolving Conflicts in Seven Principles for Making Marriage Work. John Gottman, Ph.D. Nan Silver, Three Rivers Press 1999.
   http://www.cbn.com/family/Marriage/newlife_conflicts.aspx.

## Chapter VII: Habits that Destroy Romantic Love

1. Pay Attention to the Little Things. Elev8Staff. Aug. 14, 2009.

2. Zari Banks. Dishonesty in Relationships. http://www.ehow.com/info_8653499_dishonesty-relationships.html.

3. Kerby Anderson. Why Marriages Fail. http://www.probe.org/site/c.fdKEIMNsEoG/b.4218321/k.BD86/Why_Marriages_Fail.htm.

4. Scott Stanley, et al. A Lasting Promise: A Christian Guide to Fighting for Your Marriage. San Francisco: Josey—Bass, 1998. P.29.

5. Protect Your Marriage by Changing the Way You Speak to Each Other. Wisdom for life. June 8, 2008 http://marriagemissions.com/protecting-your-marriage-marriage-message-38.

6. Financial Problems in Marriage. http://www.buzzle.com/articles/financial-problems-in-marriage.html.

7. Bill Watson. Maturity and Marriage. http://www.lavistachurchofchrist.org/LVarticles/MaturityAndMarriage.html.

8. Eight Causes of Divorce. http://www.bible.ca/f-8causes-divorce.htm.

9. 10 Simple Ways to Make a Marriage Last. http://www.twoofus.org/educational-content/articles/10-simple-ways-to-make-a-marriage-last/index.aspx.

## Chapter VIII: Affair Proof Your Marriage

1. Procrastination is a Marriage Killer. http://nottiehottie.over-blog.com/article-procrastination-is-a-marriage-killer-58567140.html.

2. Jerry Jenkins. Hedges. "Growing a Healthy Marriage." Focus on the Family. Colorado Springs, Colorado.1993.

3. Brad Lewis. Affairs/Marital Infidelity—
http://www.focusonthefamily.com/lifechallenges/relationship_
challenges/affairs_marital_infidelity.aspx

4. Beth J. Lueders. Warning Signs of an Affair
http://www.focusonthefamily.com/lifechallenges/relationship_
challenges/affairs_marital_infidelity.aspx

5. Dr. C. Curtis Brown Sr. Introduction to Christian Counseling.
Elyria, Oh. NEOM. 2006
http://marriagemissions.com/protecting-your-marriage-
marriage-message-38

## Chapter IX: Tips and Warnings for Rebuilding

1. Yinka Olag Baju. Preventing Infidelity: How to Stop Affairs
Before they Start. Aug. 28,2013.
http://www.nairaland.com/1415345/preventing-infidelity-how-
stop-affairs

2. Surviving Betrayal.
http://greatergood.berkeley.edu/article/item/surviving_betrayal

3. Joshua Coleman, Ph.D. Trust and Betrayal. Oct. 29, 2011.
http://greatergood.berkeley.edu/article/item/john_gottman_on_
trust_and_betrayal/.

4. Barb Nefer. Mayo Clinic: Infidelity, Mending Your Marriage
After an Affair. Julie Burnett. Aug 16, 2013.
http://www.mayoclinic.org/healthy-living/adult-health/in-
depth/infidelity/art-20048424

## Chapter X: The Effects of Technology on Relationships

1. Ian Kerner. Special to CNN. January 10, 2013.
http://www.cnn.com/2013/01/10/health/kerner-social-
relationship/index.html

2. Jason Krafsky. Facebook and Your Marriage.
   https://www.facebook.com/fbandyourmarriage

3. Margaret Wheeler Johnson. 11 Ways to Keep Stress from Hurting Your Marriage. The Huffington Post. August 19, 2013 http://www.huffingtonpost.com/2013/08/19/-ways-to-keep-stress-fom-hurting-your-marriage-n3756436.html.

4. http://www.womansday.com/sex-relationships/dating-marriage/facebook-and-marriage

## Chapter XI: Make Your Marriage More Important than Money

1. How to Work Towards Financial Freedom.
   http://www.financiallypoor.com/mind-over-money/how-to-work-towards-financial-freedom/.

2. http://www.maryjorapini.com/,
   http://www.facebook.com/maryjopini.

## Chapter XII: Marriage Stress

1. Becky Sweat How Can You Manage Marriage Stress in Troubling Times. Good News Magazine. Nov. Dec. 2010 http://www.ucg.org/relationships/how-can-you-manage-marriage-stress-troubling-times/

## Chapter XIII: Tips for Managing Marriage Stress.

1. Sheri & Bob Stritof. Burnout and Stress Can Devastate Your Marriage.
   http://marriage.about.com/cs/stress/qt/copingstress.htm

## Chapter XIV: Marriage and Ministry

1. Jan & Eugene Peterson et.al. Marriage and Ministry. June 2008.
   www.crcna.org/sites/default/files/Marriage_and_Ministry.pdf